A Night Out With the Boys

A Night Out With the Boys

Haydn Davies
with Linda Jenkins
and Andrew Chamberlain

Authentic

LONDON ● COLORADO SPRINGS ● HYDERABAD

12 11 10 09 08 07 06   7 6 5 4 3 2 1

First published 2007 by Authentic Media
9 Holdom Avenue, Bletchley, Milton Keynes, MK1 1QR, UK
1820 Jet Stream Drive , Colorado Springs, CO 80921
OM Authentic Media, Medchal Road, Jeedimetla Village,
Secunderabad 500 055, A.P., India
www.authenticmedia.co.uk
Authentic Media is a division of Send the Light Ltd., a company
limited by guarantee (registered charity no. 270162)

British Library Cataloguing in Publication Data
A catalogue record for this book is available from the
British Library

ISBN 978-1-85078-735-8

Cover Design by
Print Management by Adare Carwin
Printed in Great Britain by J.H. Haynes & Co., Sparkford

Contents

Acknowledgements

There are so many people that I would like to thank for helping me throughout my eventful journey.

First and foremost I thank God for making me who I am, and for providing me with such a wonderful caring wife, Karla. In her wisdom, Karla has encouraged and supported me in everything. She has never wavered, even through the most difficult times. She is and always will be very special to me. Also our lovely daughter Hayley, who is our pride and joy, a most precious gift from God.

I have to include my late parents Haydn and Barbara Davies, who lovingly cared for me throughout my life and gave up so much to support me throughout my recovery. Not forgetting my brother Alan, who because of my accident, missed out on so much but was always there for me.

Also my extended family, the Davies and Seawards, who have been so very faithful during the time of my accident and the years to follow.

To all the medical teams who were so dedicated in their efforts to get me back on my feet again after my accident, thank you.

A special thanks to Linda Jenkins who spent almost every Monday evening over two years helping me put my story into print; during this time we've had many laughs at the antics I used to get up to. Without her perseverance, this book would never have happened.

My thanks to Stuart Olyott for his kindness in taking time out of his busy schedule to advise and direct me. I appreciate his help immensely. Also a big thank you to Andrew Chamberlain for working on my book, and for his patience with my many changes. His input to finalize my book has been invaluable.

For my many friends, including my mentors Jeff and Steve, my ex-football mates, my work mates and my fellow Christians.

Last but not least, thank you to Authentic Media, especially Charlotte Hubback for all her guidance and support.

Foreword

I couldn't put this book down! Haydn is my kind of bloke through and through: a Welsh boy, mad on football, wanting to live life to the maximum and yet willing to take crazy risks as 'one of the boys'.

Indeed, one of the things I really enjoyed about this book is that as the story develops and then moves towards its conclusion with Haydn's new found Christian faith, there isn't a moment where you lose track of his earthy personality. We certainly see his character change for the good, but crucially not his God given personality – lively, real and full of banter.

I find this very important. At the heart of Christian biography lies the profound truth that God takes very different people from a very wide background and brings them into a relationship with Him regardless of their past. This is a given of Christian biography. However, what is so significantly encouraging in this story is that at no point are we in danger of forgetting that the young Haydn at the beginning of the story is the same vibrant and colourful man at the end; his new start in Jesus Christ has enhanced his life, making it even more colourful but with a greater purpose than he's ever known before.

So often people yearn for a new start and consider the message of Jesus Christ and yet are terrified of the fact that if they do trust in Him they will have to lose their own personality. Typically, the lively and outgoing man or woman will look at the quietest and most anonymous person they know is a Christian and assume that God inevitably wants all Christians to adopt such a persona. Haydn's story shouts out 'not true'! The quiet mostly stay quiet when they come to know Jesus, the Haydn's mostly stay loud! Isn't that great?

If you love sport or know someone colourful who does, get them this book and urge them to read it. Even if you don't like sport, don't pass this book by. We need more men and women like Haydn to lead the forward line for the church of Christ, and this book may lead to some new players joining Jesus' team!

Graham Daniels
General Director, Christians In Sport

1

A NIGHT OUT

June 28th 1973

There were four of us in the car that night: Gethin and Mel in the front, Richard and me at the back. Mel was driving even though it was my car and he didn't have a licence. We'd been in the pub all evening and got drunk; now we were racing down the road to the Chinese restaurant in Bridgend. It's a treacherous route in the dark; there are sharp bends that need to be taken at moderate speed, not the seventy or eighty miles an hour that we were doing.

'Mel, are you sure you are all right to drive?' Gethin asked.

'Come on lads, lighten up a bit. There's nothing to worry about.'

'Just remember you're not legal.'

'I know, I know! What a good night though, hey lads? Nothing like a few drinks on a night out.'

'I feel sick, slow down a bit Mel,' I said.

'There's nothing on the road and no one around to stop us. Come on I'm starving! Are you all right in the back Richard? You seem quiet.'

'I'll be all right once we get there.'

'We'll be there sooner than you know it. The car drives well Hayd!'

'I know! Watch this bend though. I want to get there in one piece. I could do with some food in me.'

We never got to the restaurant; we never even made it to Bridgend. Instead the car came off the road, hit a tree and fell some sixty feet – flipping over as it did so. We crashed on to the railway track that runs parallel to the road. Gethin and Mel died instantly. I was critically injured. Miraculously Richard was thrown clear of the vehicle. With nothing more than cuts and bruises, he was able to crawl up the railway embankment and get help.

It was supposed to be just another night out with the boys, like the ones we'd had together so many times before. It ended up changing my life forever.

⌘   ⌘   ⌘   ⌘

Things had been going well for me. I was living with my parents at the time, a modest house in the little mining village of Bettws near Bridgend in South Wales. Football was my life. I was only nineteen but had already represented my country. The future was promising. It was the end of June and the end of the season; a time for parties and laughter and beer. Who was I to refuse a night out? That night the evening air was hot and still; it was perfect drinking weather and so I wasn't surprised to see Mel at the door.

'Coming to the stag party tonight, Nico?'

Nico was my nickname with some of the lads. They called me this because I loved listening to the music of Argent. Their song Celebration was sung by Nico and I used to play this over and over again, much to the amusement of my friends. It was Thursday night and I didn't get paid until Friday. I always enjoyed a drink with the lads, but you had to have money to do it.

'I don't think so,' I said. 'I've got a big night out tomorrow. It's Lewistown's presentation night.'

I was one of the central defenders at Lewistown FC and I'd helped them win the Welsh League; they'd been promoted to the Premier League for the first time in their history. I knew I'd be ill the next day if I had a skinful of drink at the stag party and I wanted to be on top form to receive my medal.

Mel was still standing there, unmoved. I knew that I would have to try harder than that. He was good at persuading.

'Oh go on Nico! What you going to do, sit in and watch TV all night? You'll miss all the fun. You know it's going to be a good one.'

'OK I'll go,' I said, 'but I'm sticking to shandies.'

Mel and I liked to go drinking. Sometimes the local, sometimes much further if we could get some transport organized. We took the bus to go drinking, especially at the weekend. On Saturday nights when we'd had a few drinks and the seats were all full for the journey home, we'd get up into the luggage racks for a lie down. Sometimes we'd fall asleep and miss our stop.

'Good lad, I knew you'd come around. It won't be like last weekend, I promise.'

I knew it wouldn't be. We'd gone to Bristol with a bunch of the lads from work. We tried to do it without much money and ended up hanging around the town till the small hours. We met a couple of girls at the night club, and took them home. That took a while so we missed the bus back to South Wales. At 2am we decided to go for something to eat. We found a Chinese restaurant, then realizing that we had to keep enough money for our train fare home could only afford a prawn cocktail between the two of us. When we got to the station we'd missed the last train, so we had to sleep on the floor in the guard's hut.

A few days later and we were in the bar of the Greenmeadow; all the lads drinking and my shandies gradually being replaced by beers. With the presentation evening the following evening, this was not what I had planned.

Everything was fine, until Mel started to get annoyed.

'See that bloke there?'

I looked over in the direction he was pointing. 'What about him?'

'Well, he's a bit of a nancy boy isn't he!' said Mel indignantly.

I looked again. 'Is he?' I thought.

'You know what I'd like to do?' said Mel, getting agitated, 'I'd like to get a pint, and tip it over his head!'

'Oh would you?' I laughed; now some of the other lads in our party were watching us, waiting to see how this would develop.

'Go on then,' I said to Mel.

'You do it,' he replied.

When I had a few beers inside me stupid things seemed clever or funny or brave. So I got a pint and I went over and tipped the whole lot over this lad's head.

Of course he got very angry. He grabbed me by the throat and started to strangle me. I managed to free myself.

'Come on then! If this is what you want, we'll sort this outside.'

He was quite ready for that so he followed me out, but then Gwyneth, the landlady, came out after us.

'What are you boys doing? I don't want any trouble here. Now sort it out!'

Gwyneth wasn't someone you would want to upset; she could be frightening. She meant what she said. Also, by this time, I realized that the boy was pretty big and neither of us were really fighters; I think we were both looking for a way out. I apologized and we went inside and I bought him a pint.

My plan to stick with shandies faded as the evening wore on. By closing time we'd had a skinful, and so we decided to go to the Chinese restaurant in Bridgend for something to eat.

'But we haven't got any transport,' I said.

'Go and get your car!' said one of the lads. They all knew I had a car, and it was only two miles away, at home. I knew I'd had too much to drink but, again I was easily led.

'Car, car, car, CAR!' We were all sitting around a table and they were soon chanting at me. The noise grew, and I couldn't think straight.

'OK! All right!' I turned to Mel, 'you'd better come with me.'

Mel and I walked the two miles uphill from Llangeinor to my home in Bettws. We even stopped at another pub on the way for a pint with the regulars there.

'Anyone else want to come?' I asked while I was there.

'I'll come with you,' said Colin. Colin was a workmate of mine. He was married and although he was a steady drinker, he didn't get as wild as we did.

'I think I'll stay here with Colin whilst you get the car Nico,' said Mel. 'Call for us on the way back.'

I sneaked into the house, taking the keys from the kitchen and dashed back out. Dad would be very angry if he found out that I had been drinking and driving. As I drove away, I glanced in the mirror and saw him standing on the pavement, waving his fist at me. There would be hell to pay when I got home. I picked up Mel and Colin and headed off to collect the other lads.

As we were driving to Llangeinor, Colin spoke up.

'Stop the car. I've changed my mind.'

Maybe he'd sobered up enough to think about what he was doing. His wife wouldn't have been pleased if he had ended up out on the town with us, and perhaps he didn't want an argument.

Colin got out and we drove to the Greenmeadow pub to pick up the others. Steve, the guy who was getting married, was in a worse state than the rest of us.

While I was out of the car, Mel climbed into the driving seat. I wasn't too happy about this; I'd only had the car about three weeks, and Mel hadn't even passed his test. But he was full of lager and determined to drive.

'I'll take good care of your car, don't you worry.'

We bundled Steve in to the back of the car; I don't think he knew where he was. We'd not gone too far before I realized that he wasn't in a fit state to take anywhere.

'We'll have to drop him off at home,' I said, 'he's all over the place.'

Mel weaved the car through the village to Steve's house, and we dropped him off; then we raced up the New Road heading towards Bridgend. Mel was driving and I was at the back behind him; Gethin was in the passenger seat and Richard sat next to me.

Mel floored the accelerator, and we must have been doing around 80 miles per hour; I started to get nervous.

'Mel, slow down a bit. You know what the New Road is like.'

I was just about sober enough to realize that we were going very fast in the dark on a dangerous road, and the guy who was driving hadn't passed his test – and he was drunk.

The car swayed across both lanes and I knew Mel was beginning to lose control.

'What are you doing?' I yelled.

I started to panic and leant over to pull the wheel as I felt the car drifting but Mel drove on; then there was some shouting and the car went off the road. Then everything went blank.

So what happened? In the following weeks I was able to talk to different people and piece together the rest of that night. The road runs above a railway line. The car veered off the road and crashed into the fence demolishing half a dozen concrete posts on the way; then it hit a tree before it finally fell sixty feet down an embankment onto the track. Sixty feet is the height of four double-decker buses stacked on top of each other, that's how far we fell.

Mel and Gethin died instantly, as the car impacted the rails. Richard was thrown from the car and suffered nothing worse than cuts and bruises. He managed to crawl up the embankment to the road and get help.

In that moment I saw my life go before me in an instant. I understand now what people mean when they say that their whole life flashed before them. That was the last thing I remember before waking up in hospital.

2

FACING REALITY

When I came round I didn't know where I was and I didn't know what had happened. The first person I saw when I opened my eyes was my next door neighbour, who was a nurse at the hospital, standing over me.

'Hello, Philip,' I said, and then everything became hazy again. I remember my Dad appearing and I asked him what he was doing there and I know my brother also visited me. At one point, I remember hearing Richard's mother talking. She didn't realize that I could hear her.

'Have you heard about the others?' she said, talking to Richard who was being treated for minor cuts and bruises next to me. I knew then, from the tone of her voice, that Mel and Gethin were dead. I didn't know then, however, that my spinal cord was almost completely severed, and with that my career as a footballer – the one thing that I worked for and cherished. As I lay in the hospital bed, slowly regaining consciousness, I was unaware of how devastating this accident had been.

As I needed more specialist treatment I was sedated again, and transferred from Bridgend to Cardiff Royal Infirmary. I have no memory of that journey, but when I opened my eyes again I saw beautiful girls dressed in yellow all around me.

'Where am I?' I thought, 'Can this be heaven?'

The yellow girls were in fact the young student nurses in their uniforms. I didn't know what had happened to me, or where I was, and I could not look around because my head was strapped firmly in place. All I could do was look straight above at the ceiling. Still no one had really told me what had happened. I felt so disorientated.

An older woman in a blue dress came into my field of vision. 'You're in hospital,' she said. 'You have been in a car accident.'

'Maybe I've got a broken leg,' I thought. I was very calm and didn't feel any pain, thanks to the morphine they gave me. I kept drifting in and out of consciousness, thinking that my alarm would soon go off and that I'd have to get up and go to work.

When I did wake again I found a young man looking down at me. He looked serious, even solemn as he spoke.

'I'm Dr Cribb,' he said, as he began to describe the extent of my injuries. But the words went straight over me. All I wanted to know was one thing.

'Will I play football again?' I asked.

'It's highly unlikely.'

The first bombshell. Football, my life, my dream, my ambition. Gone.

'Well will I walk again?'

'It's far too early to answer that question,' he replied. He was cautious; I don't think he wanted to shock me. But I realized it was bad, as much from what he didn't say as from anything he did.

'Will I recover? How bad is it?'

He couldn't give me the answers I wanted to hear. They didn't know how much of a recovery I would make; they didn't know what I would be able to do for myself; and they didn't know if I would walk again. The horror of it all began to form in my mind. Life in a wheelchair, life without football! Despair filled me; all my dreams and aspirations snatched away. At the time I honestly felt that I would be better off dead. Could it get any worse?

I asked no more. Instead I retreated into my own world. I had no interest in talking to anybody, even the 'angels' in yellow dresses. I felt compelled to be macho, to hide my grief. For a long time, I did not shed a single tear despite being in pain day and night. I felt alone; a tormented mind trapped in a paralysed body.

I was not really alone, however. My Dad was there from the first moment, sitting patiently by my bed for hours. People used to say that he looked like the film star Stewart Grainger. He had piercing blue eyes and he worked on building sites out in the sun all day, so he was deeply bronzed. He was my hero. As a child, I'd often go and watch him play football; but then when I began to be successful, he came to watch me, coaching and supporting me. We were both called Haydn, so Dad seldom used my name; instead he called me 'Boy'. But now he began to call me by name, as if to show me how much I mattered to him. I know that it must have been terrible for him, seeing his once fit, athletic son like this, but I saw then, as I had never seen before, how much he loved me.

Lying in the hospital bed, I must have been a shocking sight. I had two holes bored in my skull so that bolts and weights could be used to hold my head firmly in place. My neck was broken and I was completely paralysed except for some slight movement in my arms. I could move my eyes and I could breathe on my own but that was all. The worst of it was that I could not feel my legs;

I didn't even know if they were still there. My greatest
fear was that I had lost my legs, but I didn't have enough
courage to ask my Dad. I pictured stumps underneath
the cage that supported the blankets on top of me.

My Dad was a man of few words. He would sit beside
me without speaking, just being there for me. He made
the difficult journey to and from Cardiff twice a day
while I was there. And I knew my Mam would have too,
if it wasn't for her illness. Once he said to me:

'When you leave hospital and come home, do whatever you can yourself, and I will do the rest.'

If I wanted to get through this for anyone, it was for him.

The drug-induced detachment I had experienced
soon gave way to terrible agony. I felt sick with shock
and pain. The summer heat didn't help either, and
although the nurses would sponge me down, it didn't
do much to relieve it. The feeling of nausea was the
worst thing, although I did not often vomit. Nurses tried
to persuade me to eat, but I could not; my weight
dropped rapidly until I weighed only about seven stone.
Dad could see the pain that I was in.

'If you want to swear, son, then go ahead,' he said.

But I couldn't. I respected him too much to swear in
front of him.

I remember the moment I found out I still had legs.
My Auntie Vera came to visit me. She was a very straight
and honest woman, and didn't stand for any nonsense. I
trusted her to give me a truthful answer, and I was brave
enough to ask.

'Auntie?'

'Yes, Haydn.'

'Auntie, have I still got my legs?'

'Yes, you have got your legs,' she replied. She didn't
laugh or comment on my question, she just gave me the
answer I needed.

What relief! This was the first piece of good news I had had for three weeks. I had lived with the possibility that my legs were now just stumps; but if I had legs, and feet, then surely there was a chance that I would be able to walk again. As I couldn't move at all, the nurses had fixed some mirrors either side of my bed to give me some vision around the ward. Auntie Vera moved one of them so that I could see my legs for myself. I was over-joyed!

It was not all good though. One of the doctors told my Dad that I would never walk again. But I wasn't having that; my Dad loved me and I wanted to give something back to him, some hope. I wanted to give my Mam hope too. She had suffered for many years from terrible ago-raphobia and was a prisoner in her own home. I knew that she longed to see me and be with me if she could. I knew she was thinking of me, I knew she was suffering too.

'Dad,' I said, 'if it takes me ten years, I will walk again.'

It was the first time since the accident that I had expressed any hope for the future; and I was deter-mined. I wanted to fight for Dad's sake, because he was my rock and because I saw how hard it was for him to accept that the son he had loved for nineteen years, and who had such a great future, was now deprived of so much. He had visited me in hospital on the day that I was born – healthy and full of life. Now I was an invalid. If I was going to fight for anyone it was him.

3

EARLY MEMORIES

They say that the older you get the more you live in the
past. It's true too that when everything's suddenly taken
away from you, it's then that you think back to what you
did have – to the past, to those happy memories and
what was – in order to cope with the present pain. The
more I saw Dad, the more he reminded me of my old
life, of where I had come from, of a sense of belonging.
Having survived the accident, I now gave all my
thoughts to the past – to my life and what might have
been.

I was born on 29th May 1954, at 6.45pm in Bridgend
Hospital, the same hospital I would come to nineteen
years later, with multiple injuries and a broken neck. My
Mam had a very hard time with me when she was in
labour, and spent ten days in bed after I was born. I sus-
pect that she suffered from post-natal depression; it was
undiagnosed and she would have received no support.
My birth may well have triggered her lifelong struggle
with depression and agoraphobia. She was a lively and
outgoing person who loved dancing and travelled the
country before I was born, but within a few years had
become a virtual recluse. It must have been hard for

Dad, seeing the woman he married change so much; there was little that he could do.

The first year of my life was spent in the South Wales mining valleys, in a place called Pontycymmer. The house my parents lived in was old; it had three storeys and they shared it with my uncle and aunt. In the summer of 1955 we moved down the valley to the small village of Bettws, where a new council estate had been built. The roads on the site were still incomplete when we moved in, but my parents were grateful for a place of their own.

I was quite a nervous child but had a vivid imagination, and this led to frequent nightmares. In those days, in the Welsh Valleys, almost everybody was Anglo-Saxon mixed with Celtic. Parents would threaten children with the 'black man' if they were naughty. We didn't realize then that this was a racist attitude. The only time we encountered people of other races was when we went on holiday to Porthcawl. I would see dark-skinned men in turbans down on the seafront selling goods out of suitcases. These men frightened me because they were persistent and threatened us with bad luck if we didn't buy from them. I would dream that I saw black men walking into my room and frogs running up my pillow. I would run to my parents' bed, beside myself with fear.

In my toddler years I was diagnosed with asthma, so whenever I went up to the playing field near our house, my Mam used to make me put my wellies on. Who ever heard of playing football in your wellies? I always did what I was told, but I also pulled faces at her behind her back. Even then though, football was part of my life.

One day when I was about five years old, my Mam took me to a carnival. I was dressed up as a footballer. I cried all through the carnival because of the strange men coming up to me in funny masks. They terrified me! Back at home, I had a good hiding from my Mam for making such a fuss.

I didn't see so much of my Dad because he was always at work; but he was the one who first took me to the cinema. I enjoyed the film for a while, but most of the time I was more fascinated by the light that shines from the back of the cinema when the film is on.

'Dad, what's that? Dad, what's that?' I asked, over and over again.

'Stop asking silly questions! You're getting on my nerves,' he said.

Then a scorpion appeared on the screen, crawling up someone's arm. I screamed.

'I want to go home to Mam! I want my Mam!' I said, hanging on to him.

Dad groaned. 'That's put the tin hat on it, all right,' he said. 'Come on, boy, I've had enough,' and he took me home.

My first teacher at primary school was Miss Beynon. Abrupt and dominant, she was a real old-style teacher. On that first day, I can still remember looking over my shoulder as Mam waved goodbye, wondering whether she would ever come back.

Mrs Beynon asked us all to write down our names, but I didn't know how to do this. I glanced across to the boy sitting next to me. His name was Stephen Roderick. He was having no problem writing his name and I decided to copy his work. To my horror, when the teacher came around to read out our names to the class, she picked up my piece of paper.

'Good heavens, there are two Stephen Roderick's in this class!' she exclaimed.

'No, Miss,' I said innocently, 'my name is Haydn Davies.'

She wasn't pleased, but things got worse before the day had finished. When it was time for our first school dinner, Miss Beynon sent us all to wash our hands. As my classmates washed their hands and headed off for lunch, I stripped to the waist and had a really good wash. To me this was normal. Whenever I saw one of my relatives coming through the door for a visit, I would run upstairs quickly and have a good wash and change my clothes.

Soon, I heard someone come in and a gruff female voice shouted: 'What are you doing, boy? You are supposed to wash your hands, not have a bath!' Then she raised her hand and clipped me around the ear. This really did put me off school – a clip around the ear for being so hygienic!

By the time I started school my Mam was expecting another baby. I was very excited about having a baby brother or sister.

'When is the baby coming? When is the baby coming?' I would ask, again and again. Little did I realize that it took longer than a few days for a baby to come.

I remember one occasion when I asked if the baby was coming, and my Mam said 'Not for a while yet.'

But then the baby came on the following day. I was lying in bed when I heard a loud noise; I thought a helicopter was landing in our garden. It was actually the midwife's ancient car, a real old banger, grumbling up to our house. All I could do was wait, but I was desperate to see the baby. Then I heard a baby crying and I was taken into my Mam's bedroom. She was sitting up in bed and there was a small white bundle in her arms.

'This is your new baby brother,' Mam said.

I was thrilled. 'Where did he come from?' I asked.

'The midwife brought him in her black bag.'

I ran across to the bag to see if there were any more in there. But I thought they must have sold out because there were no more babies in that bag! For some reason I was keen to call him Alan, although my parents wanted to name him John. In the end he was registered as Alan John Davies.

I wish they'd given me a middle name as well. Haydn Davies was a common name in Wales; as well as me and my Dad there was even another Haydn Davies who played football for Llangeinor.

I remember once in my teens going to the doctor's, and the first thing he said to me was, 'You don't look forty-one!'

It turned out that he had my Dad's notes.

⌘　　⌘　　⌘　　⌘

These memories came back to me as I spent long, empty hours in my hospital bed. At night when pain kept me awake and my only distraction was the sound of other patients snoring and groaning, I would think back to these childhood experiences. It was like another life, one I had lost, now replaced by boredom and pain and hopelessness. I could not even move. I was strapped down, held in place, bolts in my skull, cleaned and fed by others; that was my life now, and I hated it.

4

HOOKED

At junior school I discovered the great passion of my life
– SPORT. I found that I had been born with a gift, a natural ability for all kinds of sport. On school sports day, I
won a medal for excelling in the various competitions –
the sprint, relay, egg and spoon race, wheelbarrow race,
cork ball throwing – and earning more points than anyone else; not a bad achievement for a boy with asthma. I
was presented with the medal in morning assembly.
Everyone in the school clapped; I had never won an
award before and I sneaked out of school in the lunch
hour, running all the way home to show it to my Mam.

In those days, only rugby was allowed in Welsh
schools because it was the national sport. If you were
caught playing soccer, you were called a sissy. Every
Friday afternoon, we were taken to the field near my
house for rugby practice. I did not understand the rules
of the game very well, because I'd been playing soccer
with my friends and following it on television. In our
first rugby game, one of the boys picked up the ball and
ran with it and I chased him. When he had almost
reached the line, he was tackled and I picked up the ball
and scored a try. The teacher, Mr George, was certainly

impressed, and at the tender age of nine, I was chosen for the school team.

Mr George selected a squad of about twenty-two players and I began to learn the rules of rugby properly. We played against other schools, and although I got to play I was on the fringe of things: my teammates were all a year older than me and at that age the difference showed.

At the beginning of the new season, Mr George announced that the team would need a new captain. He had told me that I was a budding international player. I loved to run with the ball; I scored a good number of tries as well. I knew that I stood a chance of being chosen and I really coveted the honour. My rival was the lad I had sat next to at primary school – Stephen Roderick. He was a good player, solid in the front row of the scrum, a hard hooker.

The whole team was expecting Mr George to make the announcement, but instead he said that Stephen and I would have to toss for it. We stood at each side of him whilst he reached in his pocket and found a coin.

'What do you want, Davies? Heads or tails?'

'Heads,' I replied.

There was a suspended silence as he tossed the coin; it seemed to hang in the air, a little spinning disc of metal, and there was a gasp from the whole team before it fell to the floor and landed on the grass. Mr George examined it.

'Roderick, you've won the toss,' he said. 'You're captain! Davies, you're vice-captain.'

And that was it. Everyone's attention moved to the game. I tried to hide my desperate disappointment. It mattered to me so much to have this great honour. I was convinced that he should have made the decision on merit, and I thought he should have chosen me.

When the rugby season was over, I turned my attention to cricket. Again, my selection for the school cricket team came when I was a year younger than most others. This meant that by the following year, I was far more experienced than other boys of my age. I was a good all-rounder, able both to bat and bowl.

Yes, sport had been my life. I loved the competition, the teamwork and the thrill of being wanted to play on school teams. Who would have thought that it would have ended up like this, on a hospital bed, with only these memories to cling on to? This was the life that I wanted back so badly as I lay for hours on end with nothing to do or see.

My life was filled with sport. When I was ten or eleven, I was still playing soccer for Bettws Boys' Club, with lads a few years older than myself but I knew the time was coming when I would have to choose between rugby and soccer. It would not be an easy decision as I was equally good at both.

In my final year at junior school I was chosen to represent the district in rugby. The district team usually played against other counties, but I remember one time when a joint Valleys' team was formed to play against the district. Mr George, my school rugby coach, was one of the district selectors and was chosen to coach the Valleys' team. He made me captain of the Valleys' team to make up for the disappointment of not leading the school team. We played on the famous brewery field in Bridgend and there was a tremendous atmosphere, with a crowd of about two thousand. They had come to watch Bridgend Rugby Club. We were only the warm-up act, but the spectators were enthusiastic and there was a real buzz in the place.

It was a tight game, and we were fairly evenly matched; both teams were looking for one chance, one mistake to exploit. I was watching one of the opposing players coming towards me with the ball, but then he dropped it! I was the nearest player from our team to it, so I grabbed the ball, and ran as hard as I could up the pitch as the adrenaline kicked in.

I could still hear the cheers of the crowd and the shouts of my team mates, but for that moment I also felt like I was on my own. I knew that all eyes were on me, but I blocked it out so that there was only me and the ball, and the try line gradually getting closer; my legs running as hard as they could, opposition players closing in, some trying to go for a tackle. I ran the whole length of the field, the line was in front of me and my lungs were burning and at the last moment, with the line in sight I felt the tackle. I'd been brought down a yard short of a try.

It was a massive run for a ten-year-old and I was so out of breath that I just fell in a heap on the grass. If only I'd had a little more breath, a little more speed and strength, I could have scored a try on the legendary brewery field, but it wasn't to be. The Valleys' team put up a heroic performance and only lost by a few points; we left the field with our heads held high.

I remembered it again, lying on my hospital bed. I could still hear the 'Oooh' of the crowd when I lost the ball, the distant shouts of my team mates. I could still feel the impact of the tackle and the earth and grass under me as I hit the ground. These memories were my life now as I lay there moving my eyes around, looking at little fragments of the ward in the mirrors around my bed.

Thinking back, I realized that life was simple then. Sport was my passion, not school, or other activities, and certainly not girls!

Sometimes when I lay in the hospital bed, the memories were so real and so sharp that I actually forgot where I was, and what had happened. I would doze off and dream about my childhood; escaping for a while before the pain and the frustration brought me back to reality, to the fact that I could not move at all, not even my head. I knew by this stage that my neck was broken and dislocated and the bone kept slipping out. No wonder I was in constant pain.

One thing I could do during this time was listen to pop music on my radio. I loved the Carpenters' song, 'Top of the World' that talks about looking down on creation. The irony was that I was not looking down on creation at all; all I could do was lie on my back and look up at the ceiling of the ward, or close my eyes and relive the memories of the previous years. The only place where I could run and play sport now was in my mind.

5

LEARNING THE HARD WAY

The transition to secondary school made me even more nervous than the move to Bettws Junior. It wasn't helped by the fact that the older boys from the village liked to wind us up, preying on our fears.

'You comin' up to our school next year?' they'd say. 'You'll be sorry! The first thing they'll do is throw you over a ten foot wall!'

And being the child I was, I believed them; it was only when I got there that I found out that it was just a story to frighten us.

All the same, Blaengarw Secondary Modern School was a shock. The boys and girls there weren't just from my home village of Bettws, but from the nearby villages of Llangeinor and Blaengarw. Blaengarw and Bettws boys were rivals, and there were often fights. Because of my reputation for playing football and rugby, however, I was treated with respect and looked after by the older boys; I was tipped to play for Wales in both sports. The teachers looked after me too; I was their star sporting pupil. During the rugby season, I was 'Haydn' to them. When the season was over I was Davies again, just another pupil.

Not all the teachers appreciated me, and one or two of them were horrible. One of the English teachers was an aggressive bully. He used to shout and rave, and throw things at the kids, a real tyrant.

When comprehensive education began in South Wales, Blaengarw Secondary Modern was absorbed into Ynysawdre Comprehensive School. This was really good news for me, as we all transferred from an ancient and poorly equipped school building to one with brand-new buildings and, crucially for me, excellent sporting facilities. The calibre of staff matched the facilities; one of my sports teachers was John Lloyd, who had captained the Wales rugby team.

The head of the sports department was Dave Stanford. He wanted to assess the abilities of all these new kids so he set up a race between the fastest sprinters of all the schools that had been absorbed into Ynysawdre. That meant that I represented Blaengarw School. The race was planned some weeks in advance, and there was an expectant buzz around the place: no one needed to stoke up the sense of rivalry, it was already there. I was reminded of that sense of expectation again when I went to see *Chariots of Fire* at the cinema, some fifteen years later. People discussed who was going to win, and tension mounted as the day approached. I was representing my old school and all my mates would be watching. It consumed my thinking.

On the day of the race about two hundred school pupils gathered on the broad grassy bank overlooking the sports field to watch. As I crouched at the starting line, the tension grew. The athletes assembled at the starting point, every one of us ready, desperate for the sound of the gun. We settled, poised and waiting in a moment of silence.

BANG! The starting gun exploded into the silence, launching us out of the starting blocks. I poured every ounce of energy into the race, pushing myself faster, stretching my stride, breathing hard. The crowd were shouting for their favourites, and the noise was both all around me and somehow distant, just like my desperate run for the Valleys' team in the district rugby match at the brewery field. The crowd shouted louder as the finishing line approached. I could see that one boy was in front of me. His name was Alan Bishop and he was tall and muscular with long legs; he had such a smooth style of running – he looked as if he were not trying. I pushed harder and harder as we reached the line, desperate to win this race, but I could not catch him; his graceful, powerful style took him through to the line first, and I had to be content as runner up. But I was not content. Some of my friends tried to console me.

'Second from best in the whole school isn't too bad,' they said. But that was a measure of how they perceived the race, not how I perceived it. I had wanted to win not come second; I'd had that ambition for weeks, and no amount of people telling me that second was a good result was going to change how I felt. I had other races with Alan during the years that followed, but I never beat him. He was too good.

By now I was showing some talent in a number of different sports, and life was becoming complicated. I was playing rugby for the school on Saturday mornings and soccer for Bettws Boys' Club in the afternoons. When my name was put forward for the senior district rugby team, I realized that I could not commit to all three teams, and I agonised over which to drop. I told Mr Stanford that I didn't want to play for the district. He was not too pleased, but accepted my decision.

David Stanford had a rule that if you weren't in school on Friday, then you were not chosen for the rugby team for Saturday. On one occasion, Bettws Boys' Club were due to play a big cup match on Saturday afternoon and I wanted to be totally focused on it. My friend Ron and I decided to bunk off school on the Friday so that we would not be selected to play rugby that day. That was the only time I ever skived off school.

We waited for the school buses to leave Bettws, and then strolled down to a little village called Shwt. It was a cold day but we planned to light a fire and spend the day lazing around by the pond in the woods where we sometimes swam in the summer; a great past time as long as you didn't mind sharing the pond with the rats.

We had been there for only about an hour when it started to snow. Hurriedly, we tried to light the fire, but the snow had already made the wood too wet. We couldn't go home, and we didn't have our coats with us or any food. We couldn't go to school either for fear of being found out. We huddled against a wall and waited for the time to drag by. At about three o'clock, we walked back up to Bettws to meet the school buses, and then we walked home, making it look as if we'd arrived home in the usual way. I was immensely relieved to have a meal and be warm again after one of the most miserable and boring days I have ever had. To make things worse, the snow became heavier during the night and both matches were cancelled!

For me, school was always a prelude to greater things: getting a job, earning some money, and above all else, becoming a professional football player. When I was fifteen, I found a summer job in a garage and for the first time I was earning money. A fiver a week sounds like a pittance now but it seemed a lot of money to me then. I spent my time fixing brakes. The boss was a hard looking bloke; about forty years old, bald and ugly; I got on with him most of the time, but Saturday work clashed with football and sometimes I wouldn't turn up because I was playing.

I liked the work and I enjoyed having some money, so I decided not to go back to school for my O level and CSE exams and to go full-time at the garage instead. I regretted this later, but at the time it was exciting to join the working world. I got on well with the others, especially one guy; he was in his early twenties and his name was Bob Perkins. Bob looked after me and offered advice from time to time. Sometimes we'd talk about girls.

'Have you got a girlfriend?' he asked once.

'No,' I answered, wondering where the conversation would go.

'Have you had sex yet?'

'No.'

Bob was indignant at my lack of experience. 'It's about time you started. Let me give you some advice; any old bike is good enough to learn on.'

'What do you mean?' I really didn't know what he was trying to say.

'You should shop around! You know.'

'Not me,' I said defiantly, 'I want a new bike!' And that's how I felt about girls as I grew into a young adult. I liked to chat them up, but only if I'd had a few beers. I wasn't a ladies man and I didn't sleep around. Despite this minor difference of opinion I did like Bob. He was calm and helped a lot with my work.

But I was getting fed up with the long hours and poor pay. I was working from 8am to 6pm, coming home covered in oil and grime, having a bath and a meal, going to bed and then repeating the whole process the next day. I had to work on Saturday mornings too, but still managed to play soccer in the afternoons.

While I was getting covered in engine oil at the garage, most of my friends had found jobs at the big Christie-Tyler furniture factory. Christie-Tyler was one of the biggest local employers, and after about thirteen months as a brake fitter I got a job with them. I was now loading lorries all day, a very boring occupation, but my pay rocketed up from £5 a week to £7! There was also the promise of some career progression. At the factory, you had to start at the bottom, but when you became eighteen, you began working at the bench, making furniture frames, and with that came an even higher salary.

The foreman on the lorries was quite a character. He was good fun at times, but he was also a bully. If one of the newer lads was loading furniture into the van he would often get on the trailer and give them a good hiding: half in play, but half seriously. I remember one time he did it to me, punching and kicking me. It seems outrageous now that this went on, but at the time I was defiant.

'Is that the best you can do?' I taunted him on one occasion, laughing in his face, even though I was in pain. 'You need to try a bit harder!'

Once, he set me up with one of the other lads. I was loading a lorry and one of the lorry drivers came out. The foreman sent him to hide, and then he said to me: 'That Dorian is a lazy git. He's gone off skiving again.'

Jokingly, I replied, 'Yeah, he's an old man. He can't stick the pace any more.'

Dorian suddenly appeared having heard everything I'd said.

'Talking about me, were you? Caught you out that time.'

Then the boss gave me another beating.

It was a harsh environment. The new lads were tested to see how tough they were. Some of the young boys would crack and start crying and he would then leave them alone, having found out all he needed to know. He picked on me even more because of my attitude. I knew that if I hit him back, I would be sacked. If I reported him, he would be able to cover it up, because nobody would speak up against him. There was nothing to do but laugh and refuse to be intimidated.

In the end, he gave up with me and we became friends, going drinking together a few times. We used to talk about how he tried and failed to break me. He once commented that I was 'as hard as nails.' I liked that, I was proud of my reputation.

⌘   ⌘   ⌘   ⌘

Lying in my bed, thinking about these things now, I realized that some of the determination I had learnt at Christie-Tyler, and before that even at school, would help me as I resolved to recover from the accident. Some of the treatment I had received at Christie-Tyler had toughened me up, although I don't believe there is ever any excuse for bullying. But I was who I was, always determined, always ready for the next challenge.

Well here was a challenge, and I was determined to meet it.

6

SOCCER MANIA

As my passion and love for soccer grew, I became more selfish; when I was playing soccer I didn't care about anything else, I was just focused on the game.

I would really get irritated if Alan came over to ask me to run an errand.

'Haydn!' he would shout, 'Mam wants you home to go down the shop.'

I would pretend not to hear. I hated going to the shop. It was about half a mile away and I'd have to carry the stuff back. Day after day I'd have to go to that shop because my Mam could not manage it any more; by this stage her agoraphobia had made her a prisoner in her own home. I know she wanted to get out and look after us and live her life, but she just couldn't. Only now, a prisoner in my own body, do I begin to understand a little of what she must have been going through.

When I joined Bettws Boys' Club at the age of nine, we used to practise in the Welfare Hall, a community building used by a number of different organizations. At various times it was a dance hall, a bingo hall and a place for OAPs; there was a stage where singers and music groups would perform.

We were told by the Welfare Hall Committee that we weren't allowed to play football inside the building because of the risk of damage to the furniture and pictures. We played there anyway, with one of the boys acting as a lookout. The chairman of the Welfare Committee, Chick Jones, used to come to the hall now and again to make sure that everything was in order. When the lookout gave a whistle, we'd hide the ball and rush to sit down, trying to look nonchalant; I don't know what he thought we were up to in there, a football team, just sitting on chairs. We had leaders in the Boys' Club, but they were just as bad as we were. The Welfare Committee let us run around in the hall and train there, but they thought that the ball would do damage – as indeed it did. A light would be broken, or a chair or a window. When this happened we'd blame the karate players or the scouts, who also met there.

Bettws Boys' Club would choose a squad during the week to play against teams from Bridgend YMCA and various other clubs in the area. By the time I was eleven, I was captain of the under-twelves. When I was twelve I played for the under-sixteens in the afternoons, while still playing for the under-twelves in the morning.

All the boys' clubs sent their best players to soccer trials and I was chosen to play for my county: Mid-Glamorgan. Dad kept a keen eye on me, often giving me advice on how to improve. A keen footballer himself, he had played in Division Two of the Welsh Football League when he was younger, as well as representing the army against the other forces. I often asked him about his footballing days during his hospital visits, and I could see his eyes light up as he relived those times. That is how I felt when I looked back at my life too, as this is all I could do – look back.

I stepped up into senior football at the age of fifteen and was soon playing with men of all ages. I had developed my skills, collected a number of medals, and when it came to choosing a team I was spoiled for choice. One particular club promised me that if I joined them I was guaranteed a Welsh Cap. They had a Welsh selector on the committee, but I did not want to be handed a cap without feeling that I had earned it, and so eventually, I chose to join Llangeinor Football Club.

With hindsight I think that I might have been naïve about this. The other club must have seen some potential in me, so I would have earned my place there. But I gave up that chance, determined to prove myself the hard way, again.

At Llangeinor, I played well alongside some very skilful players, who of course were much older than me. These men really looked after me and I will always be grateful to them. In my first season, we chose to play in the Port Talbot and District League, because it was at a higher level than Bridgend and District. It was a real achievement then to win the League.

From the start of my career at Llangeinor I was playing centre half against hardened men from other teams in the League: it was a tough introduction to senior football. I was the centre of defence and the opposing team would try hard to put me off my game – swearing at me, kicking me, spitting, elbowing me in the face – they would do anything to get past me. Opposing players would play mind games, trying to intimidate and unnerve me; it happened all the time, but because I was the youngest some of the opposition thought it would be particularly effective against me.

When I joined Llangeinor AFC, they promised to put me forward for the Welsh under-21 team. I was looking forward to this chance to be selected to represent Wales in a four nation tournament in Germany. I was still only sixteen when the time for my trial was set; I would be up against the best players in the country, my age and older.

There were so many young men competing for a place on the team that I had to play out of position as full back in the first trial instead of my usual centre half. The boy who was playing centre half, Dai Davies, was already a professional at Swansea City. I had never seen such a fine player. As I watched him I realized how hard it would be for me to qualify. Most of the other players were much older than me and more experienced, and the selectors had told us that they were only looking for a squad of sixteen. As the first trial began, I felt thoroughly out of place as full back; I played as best I could, hoping that whatever talent I had would shine through.

I got selected for the second trial, and this time they played me in my normal position and as full back; they also tried me at centre forward. This was a completely new experience, and I didn't know what they would make of my performance; but I'd learnt a few tricks from the centre forwards I had played against, so I wasn't entirely unprepared.

Again I was selected. They had started with hundreds of lads, and now there were maybe fifty of us left; fifty of the best players in the country, and some of them wanted a place as much as I did. So we faced the last trial; I knew that if I succeeded here I was in the squad.

The questions flooded my mind. Was I good enough? Would they pick me? And if they did pick me, what position would I play? What I didn't realize was that the selectors had already decided that they wanted me in the team. However, there was fierce competition for my usual position as centre half.

After the trial we were taken back to the dressing room. The selectors told us they would announce the names of the squad, and the position they had assigned for each player. There were maybe fifty of us there, nervous, exhausted from the trials, and desperate for one of the sixteen places in the national team.

One of the selectors started to read out the names.

'Haydn Davies, centre forward!'

I was in! And not only was I in, but I was selected for a position that I had never played in before. I was sixteen years old, and I'd been up against twenty year olds, and beaten them. My dream had come true and I was representing my country! I'd be going to Germany to represent Wales in an international tournament. I was so proud of myself, particularly because I had earned this honour rather than having it handed to me on a plate. I'd tried to do it the hard way, and succeeded. I couldn't wait to tell my Dad.

When my name was called, I had to give my date of birth. When I told him he said, 'Well how old are you then?'

'Sixteen,' I replied.

There were a few gasps of surprise from the other lads when they realized there was a sixteen year old in there; most of them were nineteen or twenty.

The next couple of months were tough, with a hard training regime at the Steel Company of Wales pitch in Port Talbot. I was not old enough to drive, so travelling there involved three bus rides. The training was intense and I worked hard at it. This was a step up from the regime we had in the district league. Sometimes I pushed myself so hard that I felt physically sick; I had never been so fit in my life. We had a few warm-up games before we went to Germany and I found I could slam in the goals, one after another, just because I was running past people who weren't quite so fit. It was a wonderful feeling to have so much energy. Quite different from how I felt slumped on my hospital bed, lethargic from the medication and unable to move, unable even to move my head.

We went over on the ferry feeling like a bunch of kids at the start of a holiday, all the lads were so excited. We had to pay our own fares for the trip. I was very grateful to Llangeinor Football Club who paid for me to go.

Once the boat was underway I went up to the top deck with some of the boys. Just for a laugh I decided to lean right over the edge of the boat.

'Don't be so stupid Haydn,' they had told me. I ignored them until a massive wave swept over me; I didn't quite get washed overboard, but I was soaked. They thought it was hilarious.

We arrived in Germany and travelled by coach to the hotel. There were lots of German girls around waving at us, and the lads waved and cheered back to them. We arrived just before the other visiting players from France and England. The schedule was going to be hectic with three games in three days. It would be a real test of our strength and stamina.

I was committed to doing the best that I could for my country but I was also young and naïve, and therefore surprised to find that some of the older boys were more interested in the night-life than in focusing on the game. We were as fit as we had ever been after all that training, but we wasted it; instead of getting an early night we all went out on the town. I was the youngest one there and easily led, and so I went along with the rest of them.

We went to a wine bar and they gave us something to eat that was rather like sponge: it soaked up the wine so that we could drink more. Although I had started drinking when I was fifteen, I found that the wine went to my head more quickly than beer.

I met a blonde girl at the bar and I think she must have seen how naïve I was. I offered to buy her a drink and she chose the most expensive one; it cost £2, which was expensive then. When the other boys found out they made a fuss and would not let me pay; in the end she had to pay for it herself.

Later in the evening I was pretty drunk and I saw two girls sitting together. Usually when I'd had a drink I got brave and stupid in equal measures, so I would chat anyone up! I went over to talk to them and it turned out that one of the 'girls' was actually a boy with long hair; he was there with his girlfriend. He was very angry and I thought we would end up in a fight. Fortunately, the boys came over to help me out, again.

Still the evening had not finished; we met a couple of guys who asked if we wanted to go to a night club. We were drunk and up for anything and the idea appealed to a few of us. We went with them to the club, hoping to chat up a few of the girls. When we got in we realized, to our horror, that it was actually a gay club; we certainly didn't want the attention that we were getting! We left in a hurry, and made our way back to the hotel. We were drunk and feeling ill; it didn't bode well for the first match. Hung over and sick, I think I felt it the worst on the day of the match. I learnt a harsh lesson that night: months of training wasted by an evening of stupidity.

The pre-match meal was huge and, for all our queasiness, we tucked in because it was free. I happened to glance across at the table where the German team were eating. They just had a light salad. Thirty years ago, British players weren't so well-informed about diet and we became the victims of German gamesmanship. The German players were big people and very strong. I'm six foot one, but the man marking me was about six foot four. We were totally outclassed, partly because of their size and skill, partly because of the heavy meal, and partly because we were still hung over from the night before. We were beaten 4-0, and although I came close to scoring on a few occasions, we were humiliated.

Next up was the grudge match against England, the old enemy. This was the most important game of all. The Welsh have a great sense of rivalry and national pride when it comes to playing the English, whatever the sport. After the thrashing the Germans gave us, I was desperate to be at my best, so I decided not to go out with the boys on the evening before the match. On the day, we were totally psyched-up to beat England, even though they were the more experienced team. A few of the England players were professionals, already signed up with league clubs, whereas almost all the Welsh players were amateurs. Before we went on the field, the coach gave us a pep-talk, really encouraging us to give our all; not a very difficult task, given the opposition.

Half way through the game, I remember having terrible pain and I went down in a heap. It was severe cramp. I honestly thought I had broken my leg. It was because we had played two games in as many days and there was no recovery time for our exhausted muscles. I managed to get up and play on, but the cramp came back a couple of times. I didn't care; I'd have played on against England even with a broken leg.

We put up a good fight and we had the kind of passion that you should expect from a Welsh team, but in the end we were outclassed and went down 2-0. I remembered walking off with my head bowed and the English centre half showing me a big gash on his leg that he said I had given him. To a Welshman, you had to fight the English, fight for every ball if necessary, and I did not apologise.

We were feeling pretty low now, with two games and two losses, but we had to rouse ourselves for the match against the French.

Things started badly for us, and we went down 1-0 early on. I can remember thinking 'Here we go again! Three defeats in a row!'

We managed to equalize, just before half-time; and we went off the pitch for a break, knowing that we could still grab something from the game. We had scored for the first time in the tournament and that gave us great hope for the last half of the game. Ten minutes into the second half, the ball come to me just inside the box and I let fly with my left foot and the ball rocketed into the top corner of the net. It was my first goal for my country! I was so proud, and I think it lifted the whole team; we knew we could win this match.

Fifteen minutes later, the ball came across and I headed my second goal into the back of the net and we won, 3-1. I would have liked it to have been against the old enemy, the English, but at least it meant we didn't come last in the tournament. I'd scored twice and my team-mates treated me like a hero; I was carried off the field on their shoulders.

We left for home on a high. It was a great experience to play against these top-class players and it made me a much better footballer. I couldn't wait for the new season to start. I still had a lot to prove, and I was ready to do it.

⌘   ⌘   ⌘   ⌘

'Haydn, it's time for your tablets!'

Reluctantly, I opened my eyes. I was back in hospital. I'd been dreaming about playing football again. I had those dreams so often, although in them I was always playing with a pain in my leg, as if my mind was aware at some level that my body was now different. Then I would wake up and realize that it was only a dream and that where this great passion had been, there was now only a great big void within me. I would think of what might have been; sometimes the frustration was overwhelming. There had been a time when I had played football for my country, and now I could not even sit up.

Obediently, I swallowed the tablets that the nurse had given me. It was early morning and the two tetraplegics, one on each side of me, were being given their bed-baths. The ward was coming alive and the night staff were handing over to the day nurses. They would come to me during the day to turn me, as they did every two hours, day and night, to prevent bedsores. Sometimes when they did this they forgot to move the catheter bag at the same time, it was agony when that happened.

At breakfast time Julie, the trainee nurse, came to feed me. Nausea prevented me from swallowing much of it and I was glad when she went away again, even though I liked her company. This was my life now, and these were my companions. If I wanted to play football, it would have to be in my dreams.

7

THE FINAL GAME

In the hospital I would sometimes wake to the sound of one of the nurses speaking to me. I couldn't complain. Not many men on opening their eyes see a pretty girl standing there!

'Penny for your thoughts, Haydn,' Angela, one of the nurses, said on one occasion, smiling down at me. I tried to smile back.

'Oh, I was just thinking about my last season.'

'Did you play rugby then?'

'No, football,' I said firmly.

Angela sat down, leaning forward so that she was still in my field of vision.

'I've got a few minutes. Tell me about it.' She always tried to keep me company when she had time to spare and I appreciated it. Still, it was difficult to bring myself to talk about something once so precious and yet so painful to me – wonderful opportunities that I would never be able to fulfil.

'I was thinking about how good it was. . . .'

And I couldn't say any more. It was like that sometimes; I found speaking about the past so difficult that I would just have to stop. Like most of the staff, Angela was very patient with me; she understood, and without saying anything else she got up and left me alone.

There were other times when I was able to talk to Angela, and some of the other nurses. I told her all about my last season, the eighteen months or so of semi-professional football that I was privileged to play. Not many grown men could boast about this, and I did feel grateful for the football that I had been able to play, but still so shocked that it ended like this, so abruptly and without warning.

Things went really well for me while I was at Llangeinor AFC. The team joined the South Wales Amateur League, and despite the very high standard, we were promoted in our first season. Towards the end of that season, the manager of Bridgend Town Welsh League came to watch me play. He invited me to train with Bridgend, one of the most successful teams in South Wales at that time.

I played for them for the last few games of the season. They were a semi-professional team, so I got expenses of up to £4 a week, almost as much as my weekly wage from Christie-Tyler. The truth is, I loved the game so much I'd have turned up and played for nothing.

With the new club came a new way of playing the game. For the first time ever, I played under flood lights. There was less of what I'd call the 'kick and rush'. I was with players who used their brains; these men thought about the game, they had a more advanced positional sense than some of the lads I'd played with so far.

When we played Haverford West I was given the job of marking Ivor Allchurch. He had played for Newcastle, Swansea, and Cardiff, and in 68 appearances for Wales he scored 23 goals. He represented his nation at the 1958 World Cup. Ivor represented a different kind of player, and a different way of playing the game.

I was only seventeen but I marked him for 85 minutes. Although he was in his forties he was still incredibly fit. With five minutes to go I relaxed; I thought the game was in the bag, but Ivor scored two goals in the last couple of minutes. As we were walking off the pitch he said to me, 'You did well boy, but always remember that the game is ninety minutes. You don't switch off until the final whistle.' A huge lesson learnt the hard way.

Looking back now I can see that I was learning how to be a professional player, not just a talented amateur.

The last match of that season was against Cardiff City. I found myself up against Derek Showers. Derek was another former Welsh International, and a real handful to mark. One of his colleagues, Allan Foggon, had played for Newcastle, Middlesbrough and Manchester United. I remember that he tried to emulate George Best by the way he played the game, but his team mates weren't impressed because he was overweight and unfit. The nil-nil result was good for the team and for me personally, because I had successfully kept the lid on a great player. I learned all I could from encounters with players like these.

The manager must have been impressed too; after the match he came in to the dressing room.

'There's no more local football for you,' he said, and offered me a contract for next season.

I accepted the offer, and signed for Bridgend for the 1972/73 season. A £1000 price was put on me, a big sum in 1972, and I was not allowed to play for anyone else. Bridgend didn't want me playing for some other club and getting injured, when they were paying my wages.

But that is exactly what happened and it was my own stupid fault. During the pre-season I played for Llangeinor. I was a valley boy and missed my mates; and anyway, I would do anything for a game of football.

Just a few days before the start of my season with Bridgend I injured my ankle playing for my old team. It was a real blow, and very embarrassing to have to explain to my new boss.

I did whatever I could to get my ankle healed for the start of the season. Near my home was a place called Sweet Wells where a spring emerges from the mountain; it was said that this stream had healing powers. On his deathbed, my grandfather had asked for water from Sweet Wells and I remembered going there to get him a bottle of the pure, cold water. Now I went there to bathe my swollen ankle, hour after hour. I had only three days to heal it and although the cold water reduced the swelling, I was not ready in time. Bridgend won their first match of the season with someone else playing centre half.

I was devastated. What was worse was the fact that they kept on winning – without me. Managers don't change a winning team and so I had to wait my turn before I could play again. Eventually one of the other players picked up an injury and I was able to get a place in the team.

Our team comprised some former first division players from Coventry, like John Fletcher and Bobby Allen, as well as some of the best Welsh players of their generation from Cardiff City and Swansea City. My colleagues were now in a different class, but so was the opposition.

When I was finally selected to play, I thought I'd played well, but I was soon on the subs bench again. I was only seventeen and it was, of course, a physically demanding game. It is right to bring on a young player slowly, but I believed that I was also being discriminated against because I was a valley boy and not a 'townie'. I decided that I didn't fit in and that the townies thought themselves above me.

During the 1972/73 season we were drawn against Merthyr in the Welsh Cup. Their player manager was John Charles; a man regarded by many as the greatest player ever to come out of Wales. Charles played for Leeds and Juventus and, like Allchurch, represented his country in the 1958 World Cup. People forget how good that Welsh side was. They made the quarter finals where they lost 1-0 to eventual winners Brazil, through a goal by an emerging talent of the time: Edson Arantes do Nascimento, otherwise known as Pelé.

The prospect of me facing up to a giant of the game like Charles prompted the local newspaper to write a feature article on me. There was a photo and a glowing write-up. My Mam and Dad had been so proud. I smiled as I remembered showing them the article. They had always been so supportive.

Although I was in the squad of twelve, I wouldn't know if I was definitely playing until the Saturday. On the day there was a sell out crowd and many of my friends and family came to watch in the hope that I would be selected to play from the start. To my great disappointment I didn't play straight away and I had to watch the game from the subs bench. As the game went on I became more impatient, desperate to get out on the pitch and prove myself.

Merthyr started to score goals, and all I could do was fidget on the bench; in the end Bridgend were soundly beaten 3-0 and I never got a chance to play. I was gutted. I suppose the manager didn't think I was ready for the responsibility of taking Charles on. I was still only seventeen but I had been itching to get out there. It really did upset me, and even now, over thirty years later, I still don't like talking about it. I suppose it was an honour to be selected in the squad of twelve at such a young age, but I know I could have done the job if I'd been given a chance.

I crossed paths with John Charles a few times later in my career; but on that day I learnt another painful lesson, and it's one that players have to learn and relearn at every level of the game: you may be desperate to play, and you may think you deserve to play, but if the governor thinks you should be on the bench, then that's where you stay.

I also played against Phil Dwyer, who played 10 times for Wales and nearly five hundred times for Cardiff City. He was captain for Cardiff and one of the hardest men that I ever played against. Running into him was like running in to a brick wall. The first time he was picked for Cardiff's first team, some of the Bridgend players were laughing and mocking him because they didn't rate him. It's true he wasn't the most skillful player on the pitch, but he made up for it with sheer physical presence and strength. He proved the Bridgend team critics wrong, and was shown more respect in subsequent meetings.

I will always be proud of the fact that I played in an FA Cup match. We had to play against Taunton, and although we lost 2-0, I'm still thrilled that I got a chance to play in such a huge competition. Not many men can make such a boast.

Away from the dazzling world of professional football, I sometimes played locally in the Bridgend and District League. This was perfectly legal because Bridgend Town was in a different league from the district clubs. The local football games were of a much lower standard and I felt I could almost walk past the opposition and score goals whenever I chose.

I remember one occasion when I was playing with the Llangeinor seconds; I arrived at the venue and the opposing team refused to play because I was in the Llangeinor squad. The opposition was very unhappy.

'You can't play that boy!' they told us, 'he plays for Bridgend Town. That's not fair!'

The Llangeinor manager spent some time explaining that it was quite within the rules, and they reluctantly agreed to play. After the match there was more uproar because they lost the match 3-1 and I scored two of the goals.

At Bridgend Town, we had it drummed into us that you had to keep talking on the field all the time. I took this advice and talked, whether I was at Bridgend or one of the other teams I played with. Another occasion when playing for Llangeinor against a local team called Tondu Robins I was mouthing off all the time on the field. One of the opposing players said, 'You do a lot of talking mate, but we're leading 2-1.'

'Don't worry,' I said, 'we can soon change that.'

When the ball next came to me, I turned and smashed it into the top corner of the net; then I looked at the guy and said: 'That's one for starters, there's more to come.'

⌘   ⌘   ⌘   ⌘

'You're deep in thought again!'

It was Angela. She had dropped by to see how I was. The truth was, I had very little to live for in the present. I tried not to feel sorry for myself but couldn't help it. Time was a funny thing. It seemed like I'd been in hospital for ages, but being in one place – day in, day out – all the days seemed the same.

'Your Mam called saying that she is thinking about you, and she said to tell you that your Dad will be in later.'

'Thanks Angela.'

At least I had something to look forward to as I drifted back into my alternative world of football again.

⌘   ⌘   ⌘   ⌘

I was so eager to play football that on a Sunday morning I would play in the works team; probably the lowest standard to be in. It was supposed to be a bit of fun; these guys just wanted a kick around on a Sunday morning. Walking off the pitch after one match, one of the opposing players approached me and asked to speak with me. He told me that he had broken his leg a few months ago and that I was too rough in my tackling, and was too aggressive in shouting to my team mates to get stuck in. I told him it was a man's game, and if he didn't like it he should take up knitting.

Looking back, I'm not proud of my cocky attitude; I was a mouthy seventeen-year-old lad who knew that in games like these, he'd be the best player on the pitch by far.

Sometimes I liked to show off. I remember playing for my works team in a match at Port Talbot, and I noticed a girl on the touch line watching the game. She looked stunning with long auburn hair and a mini skirt that showed off her long shapely legs. I could see she was intrigued by my skill on the ball, so I decided to play up to it. I would do something spectacular with the ball then wink at her, and then carry on with the game until I had another touch on the ball and do the same again. I could see she was impressed.

At the end of the match one of the boys came over to me in the changing room and told me that this girl was waiting to see me. I was flattered, but, off the pitch I was shy and so I tried to play it down. I made the excuse that I was in my work clothes so I couldn't see her. I had some stick off the boys though; they thought I was stupid to turn this offer down.

There was always a bit of psychology going on in the Bridgend matches. I remember one time we were playing Newport County and leading 2-0. The opposing captain used the most offensive language to say that he could not believe his team were losing to a load of rubbish like us. His philosophy was to win at any price. I had to learn to block out the mind games, the intimidation, and the physical violence, and just get on with the game.

Before I had joined Bridgend Town, a Tottenham Hotspur scout named Billy Rees came to watch me play – other teams showing an interest in me were Bristol Rovers, Bristol City and Cardiff City. Billy had also had a successful career with Spurs as a player. After the match he invited me to his home. After giving me a few tips on turning professional, he told me that I would never regret becoming a professional footballer.

'It's a great life, Haydn.' Billy had a big, posh bungalow in Llangeinor and I thought he must have made a lot of money through his football career. I certainly believed what he said. He followed this up with some advice.

'Now listen to me boy. Don't ever join a Welsh club. They'll ruin you!'

I didn't understand what he meant, but Billy Rees was a legend, and I respected his advice. I think now that he meant that the English clubs were very professional, whereas the Welsh ones had less money and would not be able to maintain the same standards. English clubs had better facilities and better coaching.

Professional football makes a lot of people selfish. We all played for a team but plenty of the lads only really cared about themselves. On one occasion I was playing for Bridgend against Cardiff City Reserves when the Cardiff First Team half-time score was announced on the radio. They were 4-0 down. A number of First Team players returning from injury were playing for the reserves in order to bring them up to match fitness; they were rejoicing in the fact that their First Team were losing, because it would give them the opportunity to be selected for the next game. I was shocked that they were laughing with pleasure. Another lesson learnt.

Periodically Lewistown Football club, who were in a division lower than Bridgend, approached me to see if I would join them on a temporary basis to help them get promotion. I declined at first, because I wanted to stay at the top level. But one week when I was particularly frustrated at being on the subs bench yet again, and knowing that Lewistown had guaranteed that I could play every game, I decided I wanted to change. Reluctantly, because I knew that this was a bad move for my career, I accepted their offer. Lewistown was a valley team and I was much more at home there. They had little money and weren't able to pay me, although they very kindly bought me a pair of football boots. From the time I joined them we won nearly every game and they achieved their objective and won the league. This meant that they were promoted into the top league and would now be in the same league as Bridgend.

Near the end of the season, Lewistown paid for me to go on tour to Sheffield and we spent all weekend drinking. When we came back, we had one final game against Treharris FC to complete the season. We were second in the League, and so we had already won promotion. However, to win the League, we needed a point – and that meant we needed to win or draw against Treharris. If we lost, Maesteg would win the League. Some of their players were watching the game from the sidelines. The rain was torrential; it was like playing football in a bog. We all went onto the field feeling a bit rough after our weekend in Sheffield. I didn't know that this was to be my last ever game of football.

When the referee blew to start the match my nausea disappeared. I had a huge amount of energy and felt that I could not stop running. I was playing at my very best and even hit the bar from the half-way line. We drew the game, nil-nil, and it was one of the finest games I had ever played. It was a fitting end to my career. The nil-nil score line might not suggest it, but I'm always grateful to God for that last game.

⌘   ⌘   ⌘   ⌘

'I'm still here, Hayd,' Angela's soft voice broke into my reverie.

'It was a great match, the final one . . .' My voice trailed away. I was afraid I would cry. Angela squeezed my hand and said nothing; she knew full well that I would never play again. Often at night, I dreamed of that last match.

'I was really looking forward to the new season,' I whispered. 'We were going to play against Bridgend.'

Angela did not really understand the thrill of this. She knew little about football and as a Cardiff girl she thought that Bridgend was nothing more than a boring provincial town.

'That's nice,' she said vaguely.

'Mind,' I added, 'Some Lewistown players told me I wouldn't be around next season because I'd have been picked up by one of the major teams . . .' I lapsed into silence again, remembering the wild celebrations after the game.

Years later I was to discover that Benny 'Hooks' Jones, the secretary of Lewistown AFC, had been working behind the scenes to get me a month's trial with Arsenal; it was all arranged, and I would have started there in July.

I could have been a great footballer. Not just a good footballer, like some of the lads I played with, but a great player, like Ivor Allchurch, or John Charles: men who had represented their country, who had played for what are now premier league teams, or even the best European sides. I could have been a legend, part of football history, which was ironic really as all I could really think about now was my history and the past. I thought about the famous football clubs that I knew had been interested in me and the awful realization that I would never play for any of them. I would never play again. I thought about the works team, the boys who played for a bit of fun. I had treated the standard of play with contempt, but now they would still be playing, those boys would be able to go out on a Sunday morning and kick the ball, and run, and have a laugh in the changing rooms or the pub after the game, and not think anything of it. Why me? Why did it have to happen to me?

For me the greatest challenge now would not be winning a place in one of the big clubs, it would be learning how to walk.

8

BOLTED

There was plenty of time to think about all of these events during the six months I spent in traction. But not all of that time was spent lying on a bed, staring at the ceiling. Over this period I had seventeen operations, one every fortnight, on my bladder, my legs, and other parts of my body. For a long time, I was in a state of shock. I had never been in hospital in my life before. Quite early on, before all of these operations happened, a doctor came to visit me.

'Hello, Mr Davies,' he said. 'I'm Dr Underwood, your anaesthetist. Do you know what that is?'

I looked at his white theatre gown and replied, 'Yes, you're a priest.'

He gave a wry smile. 'I'm the one who is going to put you to sleep.'

My immediate thought was, 'I'm not a dog to be put down!'

'Please don't put me to sleep,' I begged. 'Let me ring my Mam and Dad first!'

He quickly explained that he was just going to use some anaesthetic, and that I would come round again afterwards.

The worst operation of all was the one on my neck. It was not only broken but also dislocated, and just as a dislocated shoulder can keep on coming out of joint, so my neck would begin to heal and then slip out again. My surgeon, Professor McGibbon, decided to operate. After taking a piece of bone from my hip, he made an opening in my neck and fused the piece of bone to my spinal cord. It was too risky to turn me over to operate, in case my spinal cord severed completely (it was already severed two thirds of the way through) so he had to approach my spine from the front of my neck. It was a major operation and I was told that I would be in a lot of pain for some time afterwards.

The procedure had involved pulling my larynx and vocal cords to one side and when I came around afterwards I was in agony; I couldn't even swallow my own saliva. Because of the length of the operation, I was heavily anaesthetised and afterwards I found it hard to breathe because of the build-up of phlegm. The physios knew how to tap my chest to release the mucus and free my breathing, and this brought relief once or twice a day. I was unable to eat, although after a week or so I could swallow a small amount of jelly. Until then, I was fed via a drip.

In hospital you see people in all kinds of pain. I remember being in the recovery room after one operation, and there was a girl next to me, sobbing her heart out; she told me she had recently lost her baby. I was so moved by this that I forgot that I could not walk and tried to get off the trolley to comfort her. I simply had to lie there and listen to her crying.

Having had this operation within six months of my accident, still the combination of shock, anaesthetic and pain continued to give me a constant feeling of nausea. Nurses still did their best to persuade me to eat, but I found it desperatively difficult. I had been super-fit, solidly muscular from head to foot when I went into hospital, but now I looked a pitiful sight at seven stone. While I was in traction, my hair grew long and greasy because it was impossible to wash or cut it. I still couldn't believe that Mel and Gethin had died. Being in hospital I felt out of touch from the rest of the world, and I almost expected them to pop up miraculously.

I wonder now how I got through that time. I was frequently depressed, but I suppose shock, together with medication, numbed some of my feelings. Whatever emotions I did feel, I hid; I wanted to show all of these pretty nurses how brave I was; still hard as nails, despite my thin body and lank hair.

One evening, a group of my friends made the long journey to visit me and we talked and joked throughout the visiting hour. As usual, I put on a brave face until they left to go clubbing in Cardiff. After they had gone I was overwhelmed with a sad, lonely feeling of helplessness. One of the nurses saw that I was upset as I poured out my heart to her.

Later I felt more positive about the whole thing. I realized that I did not need to go to a nightclub to meet women. My mates had to pay good money to meet girls, but I had female attention free of charge from beautiful nurses working on my ward!

Dad took a year off work and he visited me every day, sometimes twice a day. He would only speak once he was in my field of vision.

'How are you today?' He would ask in his reassuring voice. 'Are you feeling better?'

I felt content and safe when he was around.

My Mam, who still suffered from a nervous disorder and agoraphobia, tried to visit me. The first time she saw me, skinny and with long lank hair, she was deeply shocked; I could see that she was shaking as she looked down at me. It was very painful for her to cope with seeing her son like this. I knew she loved me, but seeing me in this state, combined with the pressure of the agoraphobia was too much for her. She panicked and became breathless and confused. The nurses took her in to a side room. Later Dad came and told me that Mam had to go home. I understood, feeling proud that she had tried to come and see me, and disappointed and sad that she could not be with me when I needed her. She did telephone me, every day. So much for 'hard as nails': every time I finished speaking to her on the phone I would cry, a nineteen-year-old boy longing for his Mam.

In one such telephone call, when I was first in hospital, she told me, 'I don't care what state you are in, I still want you home. And don't worry; you are not going to get a telling off when you come home!'

Lying in bed, paralysed, I smiled at her words. At the time, a telling off would have been the least of my problems! I had hundreds of get-well cards. Visitors came in their droves because I was so well-known through sport. Nurses hung the cards from the curtain rail around my bed; there were so many that I did not need to draw the curtains. These things sustained me. For the first few months, I was given endless attention and sympathy although inevitably this did die away as time passed. The nurses told me that they had never known anyone have so many cards and visitors. I am an easy-going, sociable person and I loved to see and talk with other people; I will always be grateful to those who came to see me.

One day, I realized that my finger was moving; for the first time in months.

'Nurse!' I cried. 'Nurse, come and look at this!' My voice was still hoarse but I managed to attract some attention.

It was Angela who came running over first. During my time in traction, Angela and I had become friends and when she saw my finger moving, she started to cry. I was so excited! I saw this as the first tentative step on the road to recovery. I thought I might be able to recover fully and actually walk out of the ward!

As time passed, other parts of my body recovered some movement: my toes, my legs, my arms. These tiny examples of progress were hugely significant for me, and for some of the medical staff who had watched my progress over the months.

Some of the other patients on the ward had nick-named me Herman Munster after the Frankenstein character with the neck bolts from the sixties television series. I too had bolts in my head, through my skull, to keep my head steady when I was in traction. I was used to the fact that I could not move my head, but every so often the medical staff would x-ray my neck to see if it had healed.

One day a doctor came to see me. 'We have decided that it is time to take you out of traction,' he said, 'the bolts will be coming out.'

I didn't know what to expect, because I certainly couldn't remember the bolts going in. In fact, one came out without trouble, but the other seemed to stick. I can still remember the grinding noise as the bolt resisted being removed from my skull. It was painful and sickening, listening to the sound of my skull crunching against the metal of the bolt. Dressings were put on the holes and eventually they closed up, although I sometimes tell people that on a windy day I can feel the wind whistling through my head.

Being out of traction was wonderful. At last I could wash my hair. I could sit up for the first time in months, instead of staring constantly at that ceiling. At first the slight elevation made me feel faint, and it was a while before I could sit upright. I felt a ridiculous sense of freedom, even though I was still confined to my bed. For the first time, I took a good look around the ward. All I had seen for months was the view I got lying flat on my back, or the disjointed images that appeared in the wing mirrors attached to my bed.

The view that greeted me wasn't too impressive. I was in a huge, decrepit ward with a very high ceiling, desperately in need of redecoration. There were about a dozen iron beds. Seriously disabled patients were grouped at one end of the ward, near the nurses' office. At the other end were people with broken limbs – those who would soon recover and return to their normal activities. I had heard different voices before, but now I was able to see people and relate a voice to a face. When I had been in traction, I had imagined what they must look like, and so it was sometimes a surprise to see the real owner of the voice. One boy was a real extrovert, always teasing the nurses and flirting suggestively, and I thought that he must be a real super stud. When I saw him, I thought, 'Boy, you're ugly! I hit a tree head-on and I'm better looking than you!'

Despite my injuries, I wasn't the worst case on the ward. I remember one lad they flew in from Exeter. He was in a right mess: totally paralysed, he would scream every night. We got used to it in the end. He had a wife and two kids; I can't imagine what it was like for them.

Soon after I got out of traction the staff said I would be getting a present. Pleased and expecting something nice, I tried to think what it could be. But when it arrived, I was horrified. A wheelchair! I had just got used to the idea that I was getting better, now this reinforced the fact that I was still disabled, a cripple. I feared that I would be using the wheelchair for the rest of my life, and I remembered my commitment that I'd made to my Dad – I was going to walk again.

Whatever I felt, I decided that I did want to try the chair. Two nurses helped me into a pair of pyjamas, the first clothes that I had worn for many months. When they lifted me out of bed and seated me in the wheelchair, I fainted almost at once. When I came to, I pleaded to be allowed back into bed. I was shaking with nerves. I'd lived in a bed, flat on my back, for months, and I wanted to go back there now. I looked around the ward quickly; I thought that everyone was looking at me, with a blanket draped over my knees like an old granny.

For all that, I had to face reality. I knew that in future I'd be spending more time in that wheelchair. I didn't stop hating it, but I was forced to accept it. I began to rediscover the pleasure of moving about among other people, rather than waiting for people to come to me.

Another thing I hated was the catheter that I had to constantly wear. Often it became blocked, which was very painful; so was having it changed. As I progressed, the doctors decided to let me try without one. The catheter was removed and I was left with a urine bottle beside the bed. Periodically, the nurse came to check me. After several hours, I had failed to pass water but I really didn't want the catheter put back in. I turned to one of the other lads on the ward.

'Hey mate!'

'What is it Haydn?'

'Do me a favour will you,' I whispered 'put some weak orange squash in this bottle for me will you, I need to convince the nurses that I've been.'

He did as I asked him, and then I called the nurse over. 'I've been,' I said proudly, pointing to the bottle.

She was a trainee in her first week on the ward, so I'd taken advantage of her really. When she tested it she said it was fine! So I was spared the catheter for a while longer.

A few hours later my bladder was so full, and the pain so intense that I had to confess what I had done. The ward sister was not impressed, telling me that I could have done major damage to myself. The catheter was refitted and I suffered both pain and embarrassment in equal measures.

Generally, I was treated very well by the medical staff I came into contact with. If I was hot, they would sponge me down, and they would read to me at bedtime and spend any spare time they had talking to me. One nurse used to tell me that she was overweight.

'Well, how heavy are you then?' I asked her.

'Ten stone ten,' was the reply, and that became my nickname for her.

'Come here, Ten Stone Ten,' I'd say. 'Let's have a chat.'

The student nurses were aged between eighteen and twenty-one, so they were around my age and I liked to show off a bit, telling them funny stories. I always had chocolates in my locker and eating them helped me when I felt nauseated. I could not feed myself at that time.

'Give me some chocolates,' I'd say, lying back and opening my mouth like some ancient king being fed with grapes.

'Come on, you're spoilt rotten!' was the usual answer, but they never refused.

One of the nurses, Sheila, became my 'official' girl-friend. Dressed in her uniform, with her hair tied back and wearing glasses, she looked quite ordinary; but she came to visit me one evening with her hair loose and her face made up; I didn't even recognize her because she looked gorgeous. I thought maybe she was a new dietician coming in for a chat.

One evening Sheila was sitting by the side of my bed, holding my hand and leaning over me. The ward sister called her and she came back crying. At first, she refused to tell me the reason, but eventually she admitted that the ward sister had passed comment that 'If you get any closer to that boy, you'll be in the bed with him!'

Not that anything would have happened of course; I was almost completely paralysed.

Over time my condition improved, and one of the doctors came by to talk to me.

'I think you might soon be able to go home for the weekend,' he said.

I didn't know what to think about this. I was very apprehensive.

'I'll come with you and look after you, if you like,' said Sheila when I told her.

My doctors promised that if I was well enough, I could make my first visit home on Christmas Day. They kept their word and for the first time in many months, I was able to get dressed. The nurses helped to make me look as smart as possible in my best clothes.

'You look gorgeous,' one of them told me, when they'd dressed me as well as they could.

The next ordeal was getting to the car park and into the car. Dad had come to fetch me, bringing one of my mates with him. Fresh air filled my lungs for the first time in six months. It was wonderful to escape from the ward, yet the vastness of the outside world was overpowering. Before I was able to begin to adjust to this, I was put into the confined interior of the car. My occupational therapists had made straps to fasten me in and I felt an overwhelming sense of horror as the nurses put me into them. It was the first time I had been in a car since the accident, and I panicked. I felt sick, dizzy and claustrophobic. I pleaded with them.

'Get me out of here! Please!'

I calmed down after a while and the car drew away from the kerb. Even such a small thing as changing gear seemed strange to me, but eventually, I was able to compose myself and enjoy the journey.

About an hour later, we arrived home in Bettws. I had been away for six months, but it felt as if it had been ten years. I had found the car claustrophobic, but now the village and its houses looked tiny and strange, like a model village. Having said that, nothing could take away the beauty of the valleys in the backdrop. The deep high-sided valleys that seemed to reach to the sky glittered in the frost that Christmas Day. I followed my eye to the top of one of them and it made me dizzy just thinking of the height. I lowered my eyes again, and concentrated on the next thing: getting out of the car and into the house.

When we drew up outside my house, Dad helped lift me into the wheelchair. Will Jones, our neighbour, came to lend a hand. Being wheeled into my house was a very emotional experience. The last time I had left that home I was super-fit, now I could barely move. As we entered, I felt that the ceiling was collapsing upon me; the house seemed tiny after the many months I had spent in a huge hospital ward with a high ceiling.

'Welcome Home' by Peters and Lee was playing in the background as I entered the house, and Mam was there, getting her boy home at last, just as she wanted. It was too emotional as we both broke down and cried.

Mam and Dad had brought my bed downstairs and placed it near the window so that I could see out. I sat in it all day wearing a collar and tie because it was such a novelty to be fully dressed again. It must have been hard for Alan, not only seeing what I had been reduced to, but also coping with all the attention I received. There were dozens of visitors, coming and going all day wishing me well and bringing presents. I think I was given enough aftershave to last a lifetime. Gran of course was round like a shot. In many ways she had been my second Mam, taking us to all the places that Mam could never take us to. And now, as she looked at her grandson I could see the tears welling up as she realized just how serious the accident had been. My homecoming was an emotional time for all of us.

That night, my Dad slept on the sofa, getting up every three hours to turn me. It was frightening being away from the doctors and nurses, but when, on Boxing Day, the time came to return to hospital, I did not want to go. I'd really enjoyed seeing Mam, Dad, Alan, Gran and the others. As we were about to leave, I grabbed the nearest chair and hung onto it.

'Please don't make me go back,' I cried. 'I want to stay at home with you!'

My parents tried to reason with me.

'You have to go back, for your own good.' Afterwards I found out that my Mam wept for hours on my return to the hospital.

I accepted that I would have to return to hospital, but during the journey back to Cardiff Royal Infirmary I was so sad that I didn't speak. My Dad stayed for a while after we arrived at the hospital but I told him, 'You'd better go now, Dad. The longer you stay, the harder it will be to say goodbye.'

When he had gone, I sat for a long time, staring at the wall. I had to snap out of my melancholy because two friends from work came to visit me. But the future looked bleak. Would I ever be able to go home for good, or would I spend the rest of my life in hospital?

9

CONCENTRATION CAMP

I was coming to the end of my time at Cardiff Royal Infirmary. I knew that when the doctors had done all that they could for me, I was going to be moved to Rookwood Hospital, a specialist unit dealing with spinal injuries.

'You'll love Rookwood,' one of the nurses told me cheerfully. 'There are lovely grounds there.'

'Sounds nice,' I thought, but what good would lovely grounds be to me in my condition? I knew that she meant well, but her words gave me an entirely false expectation of what the place would be like.

I said goodbye to the other patients and staff, my housemates for the last seven months, and left the security of the Royal Infirmary; it may have been a grim place, but at least it was familiar. During the months of my stay, I had seen many patients come and go. Now that I was leaving, I was fidgety and restless, like a kid going off to a new school. If I'd been going home I would not have been worried at all, but I was going to an institution and I didn't really know what to expect. It was hardest of all to say goodbye to the student nurses; I'd grown fond of them. I was transferred by ambulance and we also had a police escort. The convoy travelled slowly because another young man, John Wilding, who was travelling with me, still had his head in traction. When we arrived at Rookwood, my Dad was waiting for me.

Rookwood is an imposing Victorian edifice, originally built by a Colonel Edward Hill as a private residence for his wife and himself. Apparently Mrs Hill came to see the house during its construction and saw some rooks in the trees nearby, and that's how the place got its name.

Rookwood was later converted into an army convalescent home, but there was nothing homely about the place. I was wheeled through long dreary corridors to Ward 6. Dad commented on how warm it was and proceeded to take his coat, gloves and scarf off; he had wrapped up warm for the wait. To me it just seemed normal now, after spending over six months of my life in hospital already. As we went on to the ward and saw the patients, the smell of urine and faeces hit me in the face. Many of the patients had terrible injuries, much worse than anything that I had seen in the Royal Infirmary. It was terrifying. Most had to be fed, washed and lifted. The ward seemed to define who I was, and what was left for me. I was about to become an institutionalized cripple.

When I got to my bed I looked around at the other patients. One man, I later found out, had been in bed for fourteen years, and had wasted away until he had no flesh left on his body. The people here had been involved in all kinds of accidents. John, my travelling companion from Cardiff Infirmary, had fallen from scaffolding and broken his neck at the age of twenty-four. He would never be able to get out of bed again.

The atmosphere on the ward was completely different from that at the Infirmary. Instead of the pretty, sympathetic young nurses, I discovered that most of the nurses were male ex-army medics who had been in the Burma War. If the nurses at the Royal Infirmary had made me think that I was in heaven, these nurses reminded me of quite another place! They were very tough and did not offer much sympathy. When they put me into bed, I confess I was frightened of what was to come.

There was an old man in the bed next to mine whose name was Harry. He'd been a coal man, and he'd fallen from the back of his lorry. He had been in bed for years until he was like a shrivelled little doll. At first I really thought that he had a budgie in a cage, set on the table beside the bed, but later I discovered that it was a machine to draw mucus from his chest via a tracheotomy. By day and night, I had to listen to the sucking noises made by this machine.

Most of the patients were incontinent and the powerful smell of urine and excrement was all-pervasive. In the evenings, after supper, when the night staff would make their rounds, they would give suppositories to the incontinent, and liquid paraffin was often used. Few had any dignity left.

My first stay in Rookwood was mercifully brief. One night, as one of the nurses was turning me, he found that my hip was clicking in and out of joint. I had been having pain in that area for a while and the doctor who examined me said that I had to go back to the Infirmary for another operation. I was glad to get out.

Four weeks after the operation it was back to Rookwood, but at least I knew what to expect this time. I began to settle down, getting to know the staff and starting the process of rehabilitation. Dad, as ever, was there for me; my rock throughout the whole ordeal. Mam too, in her own way, was there for me, always on the other end of the phone, caution in her voice as she cared so much for the son that she couldn't see. Alan now only fourteen made it too, though he never said much, he just sat there. He never did show his feelings.

Each morning at five o'clock the male nurses would burst into the ward, banging tins and shouting, 'Come on, you lot! Wake up you lazy gits! Get out of them beds!' Ironic really, because none of us were able to get out of our beds even if we wanted to.

Two of the nurses were called Dai, so we named them Dai Pie and Dai Fat to distinguish between them. Dai Fat lived up to his nickname: he was a bald, chubby bloke and he smoked a pipe. He was always joking around. Dai was near the end of his career and with retirement looming he liked to avoid hard work wherever possible.

Then there was Dai Pie: about sixty, but still very fit; he used to leap over beds like an athlete. He said that I reminded him of his son, and we soon became good friends. He gave me my nickname at Rookwood, 'Burma Boy.'

'Come on now, Burma,' he would say 'there was worse than this out in Burma in the war.' He had fought in the trenches there and knew what he was talking about. 'At least you get fed here.' I knew he was right.

There was also Willy Keech, the night staff nurse, who pushed the trolley around the ward giving out medication; he had a huge nose and reminded me of a penguin. I liked the nurses with their big personalities; watching them and engaging in banter with them gave us some light relief from the oppressive boredom of the ward.

The nurses needed to be tough to do their job properly. They were there to push us, and although at first I hated the way they treated us, I grew to love them and I now realize what a great debt I owe them. In the beginning, I had to have a bed bath every day, given to me by one of the older female nurses. At six foot one I was one of the tallest patients on the ward.

'There's miles of you, boy!' she used to say.

Later, they would give me a bowl to wash myself. Then it was time to dress. At the beginning, a nurse helped me, but that soon changed. The staff pushed us into doing as much as possible for ourselves; and if we didn't like it – tough. This no-nonsense regime was good for me, and soon drew me out of my melancholy and withdrawal into myself. Being around them made me want to win this battle, to get better, and I was reminded of the promise that I had made to Dad and myself in the Infirmary: that I would be walking again in ten years' time. 'I'd better get on with it then!' I thought to myself one morning. Enough of this feeling sorry for myself.

One day Dai Pie came in, and instead of helping me to dress he threw my clothes on the bed.

'Get dressed, Burma!' I thought he was joking.

'I can't dress myself! It's impossible!' I protested. 'You know I only have limited movement.'

He sat there silently watching me for a moment.

'I've got plenty of time Burma,' he said. 'Let's make a start shall we?'

'But I can't do it!'

He wasn't impressed, and simply waited for me to get on with it. At first I thought it would be impossible for me, but Dai was patient, and I wasn't going anywhere!

It took me four and a half hours to get dressed that day. By the time I had finished, I was exhausted and ready to go back to bed. My trousers were twisted, my shirt was hanging out and I only wore one sock. I was still catheterised, with a leg bag strapped to me. Not bad for a first attempt.

Dai Pie had left me to get on with it, but now he came back and looked down at me, remembering the words I had spoken at the start of this ordeal.

'Just remember,' he said, 'there's no such word as can't!'

After that, I was able to dress myself, and over the weeks I got better at it; at my best I could finish the task in twenty minutes.

One of the rules in Rookwood was that if you could dress yourself and put yourself in a wheelchair, you could stay up as long as you wanted. Otherwise, you had to be in bed by four. I didn't want to go to bed that early, and I didn't want to be dependent on these men. I began to look after myself and soon I was staying up until four o'clock in the morning, and still getting up at five! My confidence was growing and I was able to tour around the beds in my wheelchair, chatting with the rest of the patients.

'What happened to you?' I would ask, and they would tell me tragic stories about their injuries and report how much recovery they had made. There was one guy who had been a soldier in Ireland and had been shot by the IRA. He had a bullet lodged in his spine. Gradually, I built up a relationship with most of the guys there. Some sat in wheelchairs all day, others were bedridden. Harry, the coal man with the 'budgie', was allowed to smoke. He used to ask me to hold his cigarette for him, but I didn't know what to do, having never smoked. I would hold his cigarette in his mouth until he blinked, as a signal for me to take it out. I hated the smell of the smoke, but I wanted to do what I could for him.

Around this time I also began to feed myself – a vast improvement on being spoon-fed like a baby. I really could see progress being made, and this gave me some glimmer of hope, and made me want to help others. In the evenings, I would go to the kitchens to make toast, then carry it back to the ward and put a big pile of it down on the table. None of the others could hold a whole piece of toast, so I would put a slice on every bed and then wheel around in a circle feeding each person a mouthful at a time. Then I would go back to the kitchen and make tea to wash down the bread. Balancing it on a tray on my lap I'd give it to them. Some of them used a straw while others had a special cup. By the end of it I was exhausted, and the patients were covered in tea and toast crumbs. It was a defiant attempt by all of us to express our independence.

Ward 6 and Ward 8 were both spinal injuries wards; I was on Ward 6 and as I became more mobile I was able to get out and visit Ward 8.

I was asked to visit a new patient on that ward. In speaking with him he said, 'I know you; I was the policeman that arrived first at the scene of your car accident.'

My stomach turned as I remembered back to that awful day. Concentrate on the present I told myself. 'What happened to you?' I asked.

He told me that he was in the front row of a scrum when it collapsed; his neck had been broken, leaving him completely paralysed.

I thought we were a sorry lot, but Ward 8 was worse. No mobility, little interaction, little hope. It was a bitterly depressing place, and not for the first time, I was reminded that there was always someone worse off than me.

I worked hard at my physiotherapy and grew stronger and more mobile every day. It was frustrating work and at times very depressing. One night, feeling utterly fed up, I was determined to leave the place and wheel myself home; a forty mile journey. I managed to get through the doors unnoticed, and took off down the road in the darkness; the adrenaline helping me to push the wheels round, my lungs taking in the fresh air. The thought of getting home filled me with excitement, but then I realized that I was going the wrong way! I was wheeling myself into Cardiff instead of out of it. I had to make a U-turn and go back the other way, passing the hospital again. As I passed the front of the building, the ward sister, who knew I had escaped, saw me and came out to catch me.

'Come back! Come back!' she called, running down the drive to get me.

'No! I've had enough and I'm going home!' I shouted, wheeling away as fast as I could. In my distressed state, home was no further away than the next street. But I was exhausted and she was able to catch up with me easily.

'Come on back and we'll have a chat,' she said gently. 'We can sort it all out.'

She wheeled me back to the ward and put me to bed. Whenever she saw me after that she would ask: 'How's the little runaway?' I was never sorry that I had tried to get out. It was just more of that defiance, the determination not to be beaten by what had happened to me. Mam and Dad laughed when they heard about my attempts.

On some evenings, I would sneak down to the Chinese takeaway to buy food for most of the patients. It was downhill on the way there, but I had to find somebody – anybody – to push me back. Once back, I would feed the other patients, although it wasn't quite so easy with a Chinese! They weren't willing to wait, either!

'Come on, Hayd, I'm hungry!' they'd call.

'You'll have to wait your turn won't you?'

I'd go around, giving them mouthfuls at a time. There would be food all over them by the time I'd finished, and so I'd go back and wash each one of them afterwards. It made a change from the hospital grunge though.

Once, when I went to the takeaway, I had been to the corner pub for a few beers on my way and I fell out of my wheelchair onto the pelican crossing. When reversing over a kerb in a wheelchair, you have to lean forward – but I forgot to do it and leaned back instead. It was dark and, lying helplessly on the ground, I could hear the sound of approaching cars. Fortunately, a few people rushed to my aid. I didn't care, it was a laugh; something to break the monotony.

We were so bored we would do anything to get a laugh. When the sun was shining the staff would wheel us out into the garden. There was a high wall around the place, but when a bus went past we could see the passengers on the top deck, and of course they could see us. When that happened, I would shout 'Bus boys!' and we would all sit there and pull faces, contorting our features and bodies, making ourselves look as obviously disabled as possible. The passengers, knowing that they were passing some kind of institution would point at us and take pity on us. We could see them doing it; they were feeling sorry for us while we were laughing at them. It seems pathetic now, but at the time it provided some entertainment and helped us all cope with life at Rookwood.

10

LAUGHTER AND TEARS

On one occasion we did manage to escape. The sun was beating down, and the hot weather made us restless. I was sitting in the ward with my friends Paul and Herbie, who I'd got to know from doing the rounds.

'Why don't we go down the park?' suggested Herbie.

Herbie could walk a little; Paul and I were in wheelchairs; Paul had very limited use of his hands. It was a rule at Rookwood that you had to have a pass to go out; we didn't bother with any of that, we just made an exit out of the place.

Llandaff Park lay down a steep incline and as we started down the hill, Paul lost control and was soon freewheeling. He picked up speed rapidly and was totally helpless. I tried to catch up with him so that I could slam on his brake; if he came out of his chair he was likely to end up with severe injuries. When I did catch up with him I managed to get the brake on, but I'd forgotten that when you apply only one brake on a fast-moving wheelchair, it just starts to spin round.

That is exactly what happened: Paul's chair went in to a spin, whirling around with Paul trying to grip the handles. When it eventually came to a standstill he was hanging out of the chair, pale with shock and shaking; how he didn't end up on the ground I do not know. Herbie and I tried to push him back in as gently as possible, although Herbie didn't have much balance and I didn't have full use of my hands. Afterwards, we laughed about it. It reminded me of western movies where a stagecoach runs away and a cowboy has to ride alongside and stop the horses!

Eventually, we made it to the park at the bottom of the hill. It was a glorious sunny day and for a short while we enjoyed sunbathing before the nurses found us. They'd found out we were missing and had guessed where we had gone. We were quickly taken back to the ward, severely reprimanded; Paul and I were banned from our wheelchairs for a week.

Paul was in the next bed to mine on the other side from Harry. One night we could hear a patient shouting and crying out. We knew that one of the blokes, called Ron, had cancer and that he was hallucinating because of the drugs. There were so many distressing sights and sounds at Rookwood that we were forced to harden ourselves to survive emotionally. I had learnt to switch off. I fell asleep until Paul wakened me, saying, 'Ron has died.'

'How do you know that?' I asked sleepily. Neither of us could have got out of bed to check.

'I'm a spiritualist,' he explained 'it's my religion. I can tell these things.' His words were frightening and disturbing – especially when he went on to tell me that he could contact the dead. I couldn't go back to sleep after that. In the morning we learnt that Ron really had died during the night.

My hospital bed was old and uncomfortable, and I had asked before for a new one. Later that morning, the nurses told me that they had found a decent bed for me and I saw them bring up the one that Ron had been using. I thought I could still feel the warmth on it from where he had been. I tried not to think about it and didn't complain; this was business as usual at Rookwood.

Paul and I became great friends. He was from the same area as me and only a year or so older. We looked alike, too. Often, when we could get a pass, we used to go down to the pub and get drunk, trying to forget our problems.

One day we were chatting about life at Rookwood.

'This is no life,' said Paul, 'stuck in a wheelchair day in and day out.'

'That's true,' I agreed. I was feeling quite low myself at the time.

'I think,' said Paul 'that we should kill ourselves, put us out of our misery.'

'That's the best idea you've had for a long time.' I had only the vaguest concept of life after death and thought that probably everybody went to heaven when they died, so death didn't seem a big deal. At least it would rid me from my wheelchair. We began to discuss how we would do it.

'We can't do it on the ward,' he said, 'it'll have to be when we go home for the weekend. We'll have to take the whole weekend's supply of drugs at one time.'

Paul was unable to do this himself because he couldn't move.

'How are you going to manage?' I asked him.

'It won't be a problem,' he replied. 'I can get help.'

We were both perfectly serious about it all when we both went home on the following weekend. The best time would be on the Friday night, when we still had all our drug supply.

I arrived home and Mam and Dad made their usual fuss of me. As usual it was great to see Mam rather than just talk to her. Her eyes lit up every time I arrived back; her son, back home for a time. Since my return to Rookwood after the operation I had been allowed home most weekends which was good and opened my world up outside the hospital. Some friends called in and we had fun together. The idea of suicide was in my mind but seemed unreal away from the atmosphere of Rookwood. Home was less depressing than the ward and I began to think about how much I would be hurting these people who were fighting so hard for me. I'm not sure that Mam would have survived it. Eventually I realized that I could not go through with it. When Paul and I had been talking about it, we had seen suicide as a challenge and I was always willing to accept a challenge. Faced with its reality, I did not have the courage and I could not bring myself to hurt everybody at home. I knew that I should stick to the challenge of getting better.

I was terrified that Paul had kept his side of the bargain. As I lay in bed that night, sleepless and fearful, I realized that I had encouraged him to do it and I wondered if I could live with the guilt, the guilt that lay beside the awful fact that Mel and Gethin were dead, and that I somehow had played a part in it. On the hour-long journey back to Cardiff I agonised over whether I would find him there. On arrival through the double doors I scanned the ward anxiously. Would his bed be empty?

There he was, grinning at me like an idiot and obviously glad to see me too. He had felt exactly the same about the idea once he'd been home for a while; like me, he had worried all weekend that his suicide partner might have gone through with it.

Paul was twenty-two. He had been a passenger in a car that had hit a wall. He had suffered from whiplash and a broken neck. He was due to have a large amount of compensation paid because of his injuries and he was looking forward to a few luxuries. But he never saw a penny of his money. A couple of weeks later, during another weekend at home, I received a phone call. Paul had been rushed to hospital and had died of gangrene poisoning. It had spread through his body before it was diagnosed. Death was one way out of Rookwood and quite a number of the lads that I got to know left that way.

Life in hospital was harder without Paul. I had already lost two mates, Mel and Gethin, and as good as lost Richard too, who was barely in contact after the tragic night out. And now another, taken away from me. It was hard not to become toughened to death. I made new friends, but they were not good for me. Keith was a Hell's Angel and Dave was a drug addict. Mixing with these two got me into a lot of trouble.

Dave was a married man of twenty-eight who had fallen down the stairs when he was high on drugs, breaking his neck. His wife, who was only eighteen, used to bring in drugs for him at his request; the nurses turned a blind eye, feeling that there was little that they could do to stop him. His long hair was dark and curly and he was skinny; like a lot of addicts he had junkie eyes, vacant and expressionless. His language was foul and he had a total disregard for hospital rules. Since he could not use his hands, I used to roll his joints for him. He would suck on the 'wacky baccy', and mumble back to me 'Cool, man.'

The Hell's Angel, Keith, ruled the ward. He had long hair and a beard, and looked like the singer Meatloaf; he had broken his back falling from a motorbike and had lost all feeling from the waist down. Keith had been discharged, but had burnt his feet badly by putting them too close to the house fire. Now he was back in hospital for treatment. Everybody was afraid of him, even the nurses, because he was so wild. He had no respect for anyone and did exactly what he wanted. He loved loud music and when the patients complained and the nurses asked him to turn it down he would refuse. I loved it because he played the Rolling Stones and I thought they were great, especially 'Honky Tonk Woman'.

'Turn it up,' I'd shout, backing up Keith when people complained.

On Bonfire Night, he decided to let off some fireworks in the ward, but fortunately, the staff found out and confiscated them. I laughed at his antics. The madder people were, the more I liked them; anything to liven up the monotonous life of the ward.

The two male nurses, Dai Fat and Dai Pie, became great friends of mine, often playing practical jokes on me. I was still catheterised, unable to go to the toilet on my own. One day, the nurses tried three of us without catheters, and I was the only one who succeeded in managing without one.

'Well done, Burma,' said Dai Pie. 'Show 'em how it's done.'

Although I managed without a catheter I still had very little control of my bladder, and so I had to wear a leg bag. This was secured using skin adhesive, which had to be cleaned off periodically, using ether meths – pure flammable alcohol. Once when they were cleaning me, Dai Fat took out his pipe lighter and set fire to the methylated spirits. Flames shot up everywhere while I screamed in terror. Dai Pie and Dai Fat knew that this was only the fumes igniting and that it was not harmful to me, but I thought my manhood was going to go up in smoke! They were both laughing but I was furious. I thought they had ruined me for life.

The lack of privacy meant that, on the ward, the most private functions of the body were more or less public. John had a particularly bad time because of this, and I'm sorry to say it was my fault. Although he was completely paralysed from the neck down, he wanted to find out if he could still have a physical relationship with his wife. The doctors used to give him a gold-coloured pill that was supposed to cause an erection; they wanted to see if it would work. One day I noticed that he'd been given one of these pills; I waited the half an hour I knew it took for the pill to take effect, and then I wheeled over to his bed and whipped of the sheets, exposing him to everyone.

'Please, Haydn, put the sheets back on,' he pleaded.

I laughed. 'What's it worth? What will you give me if I do?'

'Anything you like.' He was panicking now, 'go in my locker and take what you want.'

I wheeled over and had a look. 'Nothing worth much in there, John.'

'Yes, there is,' he replied desperately. 'Look! Chocolates!'

I helped myself to the chocolates before covering him up.

I continued to work hard at physiotherapy. I was used to physical exercise, and I enjoyed it. I would do extra therapy on my own, but the physiotherapists could not straighten my right leg. On one occasion, they even tied a cushion to my knee and sat on it, which was very painful. Because I had been in bed for so long my leg had locked. The doctors decided that they would have to operate and I was transferred to the University Hospital in Heath, Cardiff, a huge newly built structure. It was like a big hotel and very well equipped, but I was a number there rather than a person.

The surgeons cut the tendons at the sides of my leg, pinned my knee, and my entire leg was put in plaster. During the few months that it remained in plaster, I stayed at Heath Hospital. Inevitably, long-term patients get to know the staff and I became friendly with one of the nursing sisters. Sandra was twenty-six and wanted to work with spinal injury patients.

'Haydn, why are you wearing that leg bag?' she asked one day. 'Why don't you go without it?'

'I can't' I replied, but she insisted that I try.

By this time, I could slide from the wheelchair onto the toilet and I found that I was able to try to go without the bag. I was afraid to stray too far from a bathroom, because I knew that I had – and still have – only two or three minutes' control. My confidence grew, however, and I did remain free of that awful leg bag. This opened the way for the next stage of my recovery.

'We'll have to arrange for you to go down to the hospital swimming pool,' Sandra told me one day. My plaster had been removed and it was time for more physiotherapy.

'I'll give it a go,' I replied, masking my apprehension. I was paralysed after all, and could not imagine how I would manage in a swimming pool. However it turned out to be a marvellous way of exercising because of course the water took my weight.

A nurse put me in a hoist and lowered me into the pool and two physiotherapists stood at each side of me, supporting me. For the first time in over a year, I stood upright. I felt strange and a little dizzy, but it was still a marvellous moment. I had been lying or sitting for a year, and now at last I was vertical!

'Take a step,' said one of the physios, encouraging me. I found that in the water, I could move my legs and start to walk. It was even quite easy and after the initial fear of falling, I began to feel confidence coming back. I was taking steps for the first time in over a year; I felt like a baby, having to learn to walk all over again. It was exciting, but also very tiring and after ten steps I was exhausted.

I was hoisted out of the water again and returned to my wheelchair. My elation evaporated as I realized that the miracle had been very temporary and I felt my weight again. I could not live in a swimming pool for the rest of my life and I felt deceived by the whole experience.

After about three months I returned to Rookwood Hospital with my right leg now straight. The physios got to work on my walking almost at once. At first they got me to sit near the wall bars, pull myself onto my feet and remain in a standing position for as long as I could. Gradually, I grew stronger and moved onto the next stage: walking between two bars. My arms were still doing most of the work, but at least I was beginning to learn to walk again. Then I had to walk up and down a set of steps, still supporting myself with two bars. The next thing was to use a Zimmer frame onto which I would lean my weight and practise walking. Unknown to the physiotherapists, I was working hard on my own, pushing my wheelchair for as long as I could. This was not really allowed, so I used to go to the day room when it was empty and no one was looking. There was a risk of falling, but the practise certainly helped. When I was ready, I was given two elbow crutches and was soon able to walk a few steps with them. Like the end of my time at Cardiff Royal Infirmary I began to sense that I was outgrowing Rookwood, and I thought it was time to move on. I was right. The doctor came and watched me walking one day.

'We're impressed with the dedication that you've shown,' he told me. 'There isn't much more we can do for you here. It's time for you to go home.'

11

THE GREAT, WIDE WORLD AGAIN

Finally, I had my last day at Rookwood.

'Getting rid of you today, are we, Burma?' teased a nurse as she passed my bed.

'No I'm getting rid of you,' I replied cheekily.

I desperately wanted to go home, but I was also afraid of the future. I went through the morning routine, pulling on my clothes without thinking about what I was doing; finally I hauled myself into my wheelchair.

'How are you feeling, Burma?' called a patient from his bed across the ward.

'Great!' I called back, grinning, and trying to hide my apprehension. 'Back in the great, wide world!'

My Dad arrived to take me home and I said goodbye to everyone, patients and staff. I didn't want a big send-off as that would have made it harder to leave. I knew I would miss everyone as this had been my life for 11 months. However a future, my future outside Rookwood beckoned, and I couldn't wait. I had said my farewells to Dai Pie and Dai Fat on the previous day because they would not be on duty when I left. I'd even made Dai Pie a present: a basketwork magazine rack that I put together during my sessions in occupational therapy. I'd struggled with this over a long time because I didn't have full use of my hands. He was genuinely touched by the gesture.

'You made this for me, Burma? Thank you very much.'

I wanted to show him how grateful I was for all he had done for me. He had encouraged me to do so much and I felt safe when he was around. I hope he understood what the present was meant to say; I hate emotional goodbyes, and I'd kept mine brief.

When I was ready Dad drove me home. I had been going home at weekends for some time, so in a way it seemed like no big deal. But it was a big deal: I was staying this time, I was back. As we entered the house, Dad simply said, 'Welcome home, son.'

So how did it feel to be back? For a while, it felt wonderful to be away from the shabby, smelly ward and the non-descript hospital food. Instead I was home with my Mam and Dad, in our clean little house, eating delicious home-cooked meals and having all my friends nearby.

However, the two-bedroom council house proved pretty small for a wheelchair, and every night my Dad had to carry me upstairs to bed. Even worse, my brother, who was now sixteen, had to share his bedroom with me again. We had been sharing the room before the accident when I came in late at night, drunk, noisy and making a nuisance of myself. Now he was disturbed every night when Dad came in to turn me every three hours.

Things were hard during the day as well. I was stuck in my bedroom for hours because Dad and most of my friends were at work and there was simply nobody to carry me downstairs. Eventually, the frustration was too much, and so I taught myself how to slip out of bed onto the floor, slide across the landing on my backside, and bump down the stairs. It became very sore, but at least I was in a different room with different walls.

For the first week or so, many friends came to visit me and I loved it. As time dragged by however, I began to think that I would be better off in hospital. At least I had company in the ward and there was plenty of room to manoeuvre my wheelchair. There were other practical problems too. There was no ramp from my front door into the garden or onto the street and it was difficult to get my wheelchair outside. The pavements were poor, too, and potholes created a real difficulty if I did go out. And if I did go out, I'd be surrounded by healthy people, and they'd all stare at me. I thought that I looked like a freak. The future looked bleak; I was in a house that was too small for the wheelchair, confined to one room for most of the time.

I became deeply depressed. At night, I would lie awake and think about what I would be doing on the following day, knowing that it would be exactly the same: getting up and getting dressed, sitting in the chair and watching television. There was a small close-knit community in Bettws, but during the week, when people were at work, life was very lonely. As winter drew on, things became worse. The days were dark and dreary and I couldn't even open a window and talk to passers by. I found myself longing to return to hospital. At least there was always something happening there and I was surrounded by people in similar situations. And of course there was more opportunity to misbehave!

During my initial readjustment back home, I had to cope with the psychological trauma of being identified and labelled as an invalid. I had been proud of being known for my football; now, sitting in a wheelchair, I felt a half-man: a pathetic human being who had to be pushed around like a baby in a pram. If I saw a pretty girl, I would feel that she would never look at me. I also discovered people talk to you differently when you are in a chair. Even those who had known me before the accident wouldn't know what to say to me. I wanted to tell them to treat me normally, but didn't know how to begin; they were uncomfortable and so was I. And it doesn't get easier. Even now, I still haven't really beaten the feeling of inadequacy, and still don't like going out in my chair near my home. I realize now that I had become institutionalized.

One time my mate John came to see me with one of the other Rookwood lads. John was wheelchair-bound for life, and knew that there was no hope of anything else. Perhaps that is why he accepted his chair better than me. He was good fun to be with, and as cheeky as I was.

'Come on, Hayd. Let's go for a spin in our chairs!' he said.

I didn't want to tell him that I was embarrassed to be seen in my chair, so I agreed and followed them outside. It must have been an unusual sight – a convoy of wheelchairs moving along the pavement to my aunt's house, a hundred yards down the street. I put on a show of confidence, but secretly I was trembling with embarrassment and fear. The other two didn't care what anybody thought and their attitude helped me begin to feel that going out was normal. John's visit broke down the mental barrier, and after that I would go into the garden and venture down the street.

There were other encouragements. Mrs Ship, my social worker, visited our house to assess its suitability for a person with my disabilities. At first she suggested installing a lift, but the house was far too small, so after some time social services and the local council agreed to provide a purpose-built bungalow for me. Delays in the planning process and a shortage of funds however meant that it would be another two years before the bungalow would be ready.

People rallied round and were very supportive. A month or so before my accident, I had played in a benefit match to support a local man, John Edwards, who had recently lost both legs in a colliery accident. I felt it a privilege to be able to help him in this way; little did I know that people would soon be doing the same thing for me. Three different teams held a benefit football match and dance to raise money for me on separate occasions: Lewistown, Llangeinor and Bettws AFC. The money was very useful because we were struggling financially. Dad had lost almost a year's work from visiting me every day in hospital. My sickness benefits were barely enough to live on, and at this stage I had no idea that compensation might be available for my injuries.

Although I had been discharged into the community, I had certainly not finished with hospitals. My new physio, Mrs Durnley, saw me twice a week. She looked like a frail old lady but was as hard as nails. She had authority, and used to shout and rant at the patients like a sergeant-major. Everyone seemed terrified of her, but she didn't scare me; after being in Rookwood with the two Dais she was putty in my hands. I respected her though: she was good at her job.

'Come on, young man,' she would say, 'get up on that bed. We're not here to mess about!'

In time, I became her favourite; I was a model patient in her eyes because I did whatever she asked and never answered back. I liked physiotherapy; because I was an athlete it seemed like a form of training. I felt happier and more optimistic when I was doing it and was determined to fight the disability that had ruined my life.

One day, I asked if it would be possible for me to try using two sticks instead of my elbow crutches. To my great relief she looked pleased.

'Well, it is good to have a patient who wants to get on!' she said. 'I usually have to push people to move on to new things.'

She picked up the sticks to demonstrate the correct way to use them. Then she handed them to me and I struggled to copy her. It didn't take long for me to master using them, and soon another barrier was broken down. It wasn't long before I was able to move around with just one stick.

I was pleased when, after one physiotherapy session, Mrs Durnley said, 'You're discharged. I've done all I can for you.'

Leaning on my one stick and feeling more fit than I had in a long while, I grinned at her.

'I'll miss you,' I said. She reddened, not used to signs of affection from her patients. Then I added, 'But I won't miss travelling here twice a week in an ambulance that's sometimes an hour early or two hours late, touring the district and picking up and dropping off patients.' There had been times when I'd got there so late I'd only had time for ten minutes of physiotherapy.

'Well, don't forget to keep up the exercise at home,' she said sternly, embarrassed at the flirtatious glint in my eye. I knew how to charm the ladies and often used this to my advantage.

'I will, and . . . thanks!'

Ever since the accident I'd had reservations about driving again. To actually get to the point where I could even think about the possibility of driving was an achievement in itself. To drive again would bring those haunting memories back, but I knew that I had to get on with my life, and I needed the mobility. Because I'd had

such a serious accident, I'd had my driving licence with-
drawn and I had to take my driving test again. In the
meantime, social services gave me an old-fashioned,
three-wheeled invalid carriage. I nicknamed it my
'Noddy car'.

With much coaxing from family and friends, I agreed
to try it out, if only to get out of the house. It was like a
blue fibreglass box on three wheels with sliding doors
and a steering control that reminded me of the handles
of a motorbike. I was a learner driver again and had to
have L plates on my vehicle. At least I didn't have to
have a qualified driver sitting with me. Whenever I was
driving it, I held my head down as low as possible
because I didn't want anybody to recognize me. I felt
humiliated to be seen out in this thing.

Having said that, I enjoyed the freedom it gave me
and it was capable of a respectable 70 miles per hour.
Taking passengers was forbidden, but I had no qualms
about breaking that rule. In fact, I must have broken
every rule in the book. One day, my cousin Gino decided to go for a walk up Moelgilau, one of the mountains
near where we live.

'Jump in,' I said, 'I'll take you up there.'

He climbed in beside me and we set off up the mountain track. It was very rough terrain and the little car
bounced and rattled as we ascended. There were a few
moments when I did wonder whether we would actually make it. We got there eventually though. Once at the
top we admired the view and I savoured the sense of
achievement. Drawing in the fresh mountain air I felt
like we had climbed Everest! I hadn't been this far since
the accident, and I had forgotten just how beautiful the
Welsh valleys and surroundings were.

Getting up there was easy, but coming down was
pretty scary. We screamed with laughter as the car

careened down the track, almost overturning three times. It was a great day's rallying.

On another day, I decided to explore the roads further afield. Approaching Pontypridd, I lost my bearings, and turned onto the motorway. A bus sounded its horn and flashed its lights; for a moment I didn't understand why: I'd forgotten that I wasn't allowed to drive it on motorways. When I realized what I had done, I was terrified that the police would catch up with me.

'I'd better do a U-turn and go back!' I thought wildly. Fortunately, common sense took over and I decided it might be wiser to go off at the next exit.

Having the car also meant that I could get to the pub again. I started going to the Oddfellows pub in Bettws, both afternoon and night, just for the company. I would have a few drinks and then drive home tipsy; the beer did not mix well with my medication. I hoped that the police wouldn't breathalyse someone who was driving a car like mine! However such thoughts didn't deter me in any way.

As well as arranging for me to get a new home, Mrs Ship, the social worker, also made another suggestion.

'Have you considered trying to get compensation for your injuries?'

'What's *compensation*?' I asked.

If Mrs Ship was surprised at my naivety, she didn't show it. 'You may be able to claim payment for your injuries from the car insurers,' she said. 'I'll look into it.'

Legal aid was arranged for me, and before long, a young solicitor visited me at home.

'I think you have a strong case,' he told me, 'If you place the blame entirely on the driver you would probably be awarded a large sum, perhaps £60,000.'

'How much?' I was staggered. This was a very large sum of money. However, I knew that I couldn't do it, especially since Mel was no longer around to defend himself. I couldn't do this to him.

'It was just a night out that ended in tragedy,' I said, 'Mel was not to blame.'

The truth was that I blamed myself for the accident. It was my car and I felt that I should have been the one driving. In fact, I thought that my horrific injuries were some punishment for what had happened.

'He wasn't even a qualified driver and he was driving too fast,' the solicitor reminded me.

'We were all drunk,' I replied, speaking up on Mel's behalf. 'We all behaved like idiots.'

'Well, if that's the case, you will lose up to two thirds of the possible compensation, but it is still worth trying.'

When I submitted my claim the insurance company offered me £10,000. I would have been happy with this, but my solicitor advised me to turn it down.

'I think you could get around £30,000 if you went to court,' he told me. 'It would be an ordeal, though, because you would have to face cross-examination. And there is always the possibility that you would lose the case all together.'

Following his advice, I refused the first offer. They increased their offer to just under £20,000 and my solicitor advised me to accept. This was not enough to set me up for life, but it was still a large amount in those days; a cheap house locally might cost only £1,000 and the average price of a house in Wales was about £10,000. I felt like a millionaire. Many of my friends were earning £15 a week, and I was going to get more than a thousand times that – in one lump sum.

My first priority was to give some money to my parents as they had given up so much to care for me; I also wanted to buy a second-hand car for my brother. Then I put several thousand pounds into a savings account and bought myself a new car. I had been longing for a car of my own: the Noddy car drew attention to my disability and I wanted to regain some dignity. The rest of the money I spent on a four-year spending spree, trying to recapture some of the carefree youth that I had lost between the ages of nineteen and twenty-two.

Now that I had a new car, I had to re-apply for my licence. Dressed in my best suit, I had to go to Cardiff for an assessment at the Welsh office; I hoped that this would help impress them. I knew that they could make me re-try my driving test, something I really did not want to do, so I exaggerated my physical capabilities as much as I could.

'How far can you walk?' they asked.

'Oh, miles,' I replied vaguely.

'Can you move your legs?'

'Easily.'

I thought I had fooled them, but they wrote me a letter telling me that I'd have to re-sit my test.

With my driving test now imminent, I arranged to try out a Mini automatic. As I was only capable of driving a car with automatic transmission or hand-controls, I wanted an automatic gearbox because it looked 'normal'. My right foot is not strong enough to manage the accelerator, but I learned that it was OK to drive using only my left foot to control both pedals.

With the delivery of my new car, I went out to practise driving in the quiet road outside my house. I was already a qualified driver, I told myself, it didn't matter that I had not yet retaken the test. Soon I felt bored, and decided to sneak down to the pub while my Mam wasn't looking. I wanted to show off the new Mini to my friends. I was supposed to have somebody with me when I drove, but this didn't stop me. Entering the pub, I spotted some friends having a pint or two.

'Hey lads, come and see my new motor,' I said. Five of them crowded around to admire my gleaming, cherry-red car.

One of them was my mate Billy. 'Will you sit with me so we can go for a spin?' I asked.

'OK,' he replied and jumped into the passenger seat. Three of the others were still standing between the car and the pub wall. To this day, I don't understand what happened next. I was not familiar with the controls so I possibly put the car into drive instead of reverse. All I know is that I drove the car straight into a wall! Miraculously, I did not hit anybody. The car rebounded and hit the wall repeatedly until I thought to switch off the ignition. Shocked and horrified, I got out to view the damage. The car had been at a slight angle and the front and one wing were severely damaged. I was in trouble again!

Billy sat in silence with me while I drove home and went inside to explain to Mam. Billy made a sharp exit, while Mam let me know in no uncertain terms what she thought.

'You irresponsible idiot! Don't you ever learn?' she asked. 'Your Dad will be so angry! If you don't get this car sorted before he comes home, you'll be in all kinds of trouble!'

I'm still thankful to her today, for helping me get the car into a garage for repair within the hour. Dad did tell me off, in his quiet way, and I felt guilty and ashamed, as I had already put them through so much. It cost me about £300 to have that car repaired; a considerable amount, and in my eyes, it was never the same again.

Test day did approach, and, realizing that it can be difficult to pass the test a second time, I tried hard to eradicate any bad habits I might have developed.

I couldn't believe my luck when I recognized the same examiner who had passed me three years before.

As he handed me my certificate and told me that I had passed, I thanked him and reminded him of our first meeting.

'I must be one of the few people who have passed their driving test twice,' I said. 'It's great to have my independence again and know that I can go wherever I want.'

'I do remember you,' he replied. 'Take more care next time, won't you?'

And for a while, I did.

12

BACK WITH THE LADS

I had money but I still wanted to work.

Before the accident, I'd worked at Christie-Tyler, the furniture makers, and one day the owner of the firm, Mr George Williams, came to visit me at home.

'There will always be a job for you at Christie-Tyler, Haydn' he said. 'When you are ready, come back to work and we'll find you a suitable job. Take your time. You can work as many hours as you choose, even if it is only one day a week.'

He was a very kind man, but he had an aura about him; a visit from him was like royalty. Immaculately dressed in a tailored suit and wearing a gold pocket watch, he was probably in his late sixties, and he looked like an old style proprietor. He went everywhere in a chauffeur-driven Bentley. I had heard that he was a millionaire and that he had been awarded an OBE for his services to industry. One of the factory managers told me later that he would come and ask questions about shop floor workers; apparently he was very difficult to fool. He had checked up on me and found out that, although I had many faults, I was always hard-working.

When I was fit enough, I returned to work. I did a few hours a week, gradually building up to full time. Every time George Williams visited the factory he came to see me; all the other lads were kind to me too. One day, I asked the works manager to make an appointment for me with the managing director of the factory.

'Why do you want to see him?' he asked.

'I find it hard to get up at six-thirty,' I admitted. 'It takes me so long to get going in the morning. I don't know if I can carry on starting work at half-past seven. If it's possible, could I take reduced pay and start at nine?'

The works manager passed on my request to senior management, and an answer came back straight away.

'Tell Haydn that he can start and finish when he chooses.' So I did, and they still paid me as if I had started at the earlier time. I didn't want people to think that I was having an easy ride with these flexible working hours. Luckily my work mates were very sympathetic and this didn't cause any tension between us. They were able to see first-hand how exhausted I was getting and were pleased for me.

The company also offered me a job in the office, although I didn't want it.

'Office workers are toffee-nosed,' I thought. 'I want to be one of the boys.'

So instead, I did light work on the shop floor, putting screws in holes. It was great to get back among my work mates and to be doing something useful. Working was tough, because I was not very strong yet, but we had a lot of fun.

We found our own way to solve any problems that came up with regards my condition. For example, it was a long way to the canteen, and so the boys found an old pram to transport me there. They would pick me up and throw me in. When we arrived at the canteen, I would look out of my pram, grin and say 'Two rusks please,' much to the amusement of the canteen staff.

One day, however, the pram hit a bump and I was thrown out and hit my head on the concrete floor. I never rode in it again.

In the factory we had to work hard, because we were paid a bonus once we had passed our targets. As the work was repetitive we would laugh and joke to relieve the boredom. Compared to the unrelieved monotony of spending hours alone at home I didn't mind, and felt very grateful to be working again.

'This factory is like Butlins,' I told the boys. 'We have so many laughs.'

There were plenty of pranks, too. The lads would go into the field next door to catch mice and we built a cage on the shop floor and tamed them. Fire extinguishers were often set off deliberately and the factory floor covered in foam. My friend Dai Eye (so called because he had only one eye) used to give me a piggy back if I could not manage to walk; we joked that he was my legs and I was his eye.

When we went to the pub he used to take out his glass eye and put it in his drink.

'I'm making sure I keep an eye on my drink,' he said, winking with his good eye.

Christie-Tyler gave the highest rates of pay in the area at that time, and my wages, together with the compensation that I received meant that I had plenty of money. Bank rates were high and the interest paid on my compensation would have provided an adequate income, without my needing to touch the capital. After struggling to make ends meet for two years after my accident I now had plenty of money to spend. I had thought that having money would make me happy; certainly it made life easier, although I wouldn't say that money in itself made me any happier.

I gave my mother £10 a week for my board and lodging but the rest of my money was my own, to waste if I chose – and I did waste a lot of it. Cash seemed like Monopoly money to me; I'd lost any real sense of its value. I became a 'weekend alcoholic', spending about £50 every Saturday night and drinking heavily from Friday to Sunday. The hangover would last until Thursday.

My friends spent much less than I did, so I bought them drinks and lent them money. I would also buy twenty or thirty bingo tickets just to give away. I didn't play bingo myself; I thought it was boring. When the *Football Echo* seller came, I'd buy most of his papers and give them away too. I loved the tension and excitement of playing cards, and often gambled on the outcome. In fact, I would spoil the game for the others because I had too much money to play with. Some of them used their wives' housekeeping money because I kept putting up the stakes: this was the only way that they could afford to stay in the game.

By now I was also betting large sums on the horses every Saturday. It didn't matter much to me whether I won or lost; I could afford to lose the money. But winning gave me the emotional 'high' that I craved. I was forever looking for a replacement for my beloved soccer and for a while, betting on horses filled the void; but even that got boring after a while.

Now that I had regained my confidence, I decided it was time to invest in a flashy car. My Mini no longer interested me. Visiting the Ford showroom in Bridgend, I was attracted to the Cortina 2000E. It was a top of the range model: bright orange with a black roof; a finelooking machine and I knew straight away that I had to have it. It was a jumbo jet compared with my Mini and was one of the coolest cars around. I paid £3,300 in cash for it and loved the attention that it brought.

'I'm the kiddie,' I thought, driving around in this great, powerful, sporty car; but it only took one simple experience to bring me back down to despair.

I had driven to Lewistown to watch some friends training for the next football season. When I arrived and saw them playing, I looked at my big, posh car and realized that it meant nothing to me. They were doing the one thing that I could never do again. All of the passion I had had to play football, all of the talent I had. Wasted. I had been just sixteen and played for my country at under-21 level. If the accident hadn't happened how far would my career have taken me? What teams would I have played for? Surely I'd have been with a premier league team before long, or maybe one of the big teams in Europe; and I'd have got a full cap with the senior national side.

Thinking about these things, I know I'd have given up the car twenty times over to have been on the field training with my old team mates again. But I knew that I couldn't spend my life thinking 'What if?' I had to live life now.

I still spent time with some of the lads from the football teams I'd played with. It's a tradition for teams to have a weekend away at Easter and the Lewistown squad had booked a trip to Sheffield and invited me to go with them. After much thought and discussion, I decided to accept. This was my first real venture away from home since my accident, and the boys were pleased that I was going with them. They were honest enough to admit that they would not be fit to look after themselves, let alone me! It was the customary drinking tour heralding the approaching end of the season, and my parents were not too happy that I wanted to go.

We got on the bus for the trip to Sheffield, and the beer flowed freely. The crates of beers stashed in the boot didn't remain there for long. Since I had limited control of my bladder, I had to use my urine bottle on the bus. This was extremely difficult, because I ended up sharing the bottle with about another thirty people! There were no toilets on the bus, and not many places to stop en-route; all the lads kept using my bottle because they had drunk so much beer and needed to go desperately. The result was that I had a few narrow escapes when it wasn't available at the moment I needed it.

Our hotel rooms were fairly basic, but then not all hotels will accept a bunch of football lads out for the weekend. We got drunk and we thought we were having fun with our stupid behaviour. A friend Gersh and I got peckish in the middle of the night, and so we ventured down to the kitchen in our underwear and helped ourselves to some meat from the fridge. For some reason, we took raw eggs back to the room with us. Another one of the lads, Les, was lying on the floor in a drunken stupor and I smashed the eggs all over his face. He didn't feel a thing. When he woke in the morning, sick and hung over, he wondered what the horrible smell was – the eggs had dried on his face.

During the tour it snowed. This was the first time that I had ever seen snow at Easter. It was bitterly cold and while we were travelling home, the bus heater broke down, making the journey uncomfortable. My parents were relieved when I arrived home, safe and sound. And though I felt safe going to sleep in my own bed, the alcohol soon took its toll. I woke in the early hours sweating and hallucinating, and saw an evil-faced red creature with horns and a pitchfork.

'Go away!' I shrieked, terrified, but it was still there. I buried my head in the pillow, still screaming in terror, and then I threw my urine bottle at it. The bedroom door opened and Mam stood there, wrapping her dressing gown around her.

'What on earth is the matter, boy?'

I told her, and seeing my terror, Mam tried to tell me that there was nobody there.

'I can see it! I can see it!' I insisted. 'It won't go away! It's the devil!'

This continued until the middle of the following day, and even after it went, I was very frightened that it would return. It was a horrible experience.

Soon after Easter, my new bungalow was ready and we were able to move in. Purpose-built, it was all on one level with wide doors and excellent wheelchair access and I had my own bathroom with all the aids I needed.

Patio doors from my bedroom led into the garden and a paved area, where I spent many days lazing in the sun. I felt that at last, four years after the accident, I was regaining some independence. Of course, my parents and my brother lived there with me, as I wasn't able to cook or do any housework for myself. They occupied one end of the large bungalow and I had the other.

Despite all this luxury and the care I received from my parents, I still continued to get into trouble during my drunken weekends. I struck up a deal with my brother, who was seventeen at the time, and had just passed his driving test. He could have my brand-new Cortina at weekends as long as he was my chauffeur. This suited us both, because he liked to show off in the new car and I could go wherever I wanted and still drink. Alan drew the short straw though because he would often be out at four in the morning picking up me and my mates from nightclubs, Chinese restaurants and the like.

The more I drank, the more I wanted to drink, until I could not get through a weekend without getting paralytic. This was the only way I could cope. Forever on the lookout for excitement, I did not really care what stupid pranks I performed as long as they livened things up, as long as I was counted as one of the lads.

One night, I was out with some friends at an Indian restaurant. My brother took us down there in the Cortina and we were all drunk. I went into the toilets and for some reason decided to rip out the pipes. I wrenched them away from the wall and water started gushing everywhere. To this day I don't know why I did such a crazy thing. As the water poured on the floor, I sobered up a bit. Realizing what I had done, I rushed out of the toilet as best I could and shouted 'Better make a sharp exit boys!'

Not stopping to wait for them, I headed straight for the door, shoving tables and spilling meals as I tried to run out of the restaurant.

'Get the car! Quick!' I called to my brother.

The lads jumped in, and I dived into the back seat as two waiters ran out of the restaurant wielding meat cleavers and shouting after us. The car screeched away while my legs were still hanging out of the back door. I never went to that restaurant again.

When my brother left school, I had arranged for him to have a job on the loading bay in the factory where I worked. This was one of the lowest paid jobs in the factory and Alan struggled to manage on his pay. When he was short of cash I would send him on errands.

One Saturday afternoon he called in to see if I'd won any money on the horses. I'd had no winners, but there was one race left so I sent Alan to the bookies. My horse won the race and so I was glad to be able to share the winnings. As a result of my accident, Alan had not had a normal upbringing and had been deprived of my parents' attention. I felt sorry for him and I think I was trying to make up for it by giving him money. I knew it could never really replace my parents' attention but it was all I could offer him.

13

DANCING WITH KARLA

By the start of 1976, I was almost independent, and I'd made as much recovery as I was ever going to. From being almost completely paralysed, I was now about as disabled as someone with a broken leg; I could even walk without sticks for short distances.

Still only twenty-two, I had spent the previous three years in hospital or recovering. As a result of this I had lost all confidence and felt that no girl would even look at me. I was amazed, therefore, when I found it quite easy to get a girlfriend. I wondered whether they went out with me because they felt sorry for me, or because I had plenty of money. I couldn't tell. I didn't think that they actually liked me as a person and so often put on a front. The rather blunt approach to chat-up lines still remained though; I'd get straight to the point.

'Get your coat, love. We're off!' That was a favourite.

I never stayed with any girl for long and I thought courting was the most boring thing in the world. It was much more fun going out with the boys and getting into mischief. Occasionally, I would find a girl to take home at the end of the evening, but the next day, when I was sober, I would not remember who she was; I'd even struggle to remember her name.

This was my life, for about two years: light duties at Christie-Tyler, lots of drinking, lots of chatting up girls and no commitments; and that suited me just fine. I had no desire to change the way I lived, or the way I treated girls; I was one of the lads.

It was Christmas Eve, 1978, and I was at the local disco as usual. As I walked in a girl called Pat, who I knew quite well, called out to me.

'Come and have a dance with me.'

'Later,' I replied. I was still sober and I needed a few drinks to dull my senses and build up the courage to dance. I spent the evening doing what I did best – joking with the lads and drinking. Just before the end of the night I remembered Pat and staggered over to where she had been sitting. She wasn't there any longer, but her friend was.

'Tell Pat I kept my promise,' I said to this girl, 'I came over to dance with her.'

'If you can dance with her, why can't you dance with me?' she asked, smiling.

So I did. I discovered that her name was Karla, and she discovered that I was so drunk I would fall over if she didn't hold on to me. I had seen her before and thought she was about eighteen, far too young for me; I was twenty-four. I was sober enough to notice that she was curvaceous, with dark hair and beautiful large brown eyes.

'When she's a bit older and has lost her puppy fat, she'll be a really lovely girl,' I thought, much to my dismay now. Because she had asked me to dance, I decided that she must be interested in me. With my usual bravado I tried my favourite chat-up line: 'Get your coat, I'm taking you home.'

'You can't take me home,' she replied. 'You're too drunk to drive, and anyway, I've already arranged to share a taxi with some friends.'

'I have a car waiting outside,' I said, knowing that as usual my brother was waiting to chauffeur me home. Karla looked at me dubiously. She was not very keen on the idea of going home with a drunk, chaperoned by his brother. I was persistent, though, and she gave in.

When we arrived at her home, I followed her out of the car. She was so tiny that, even standing on the kerb, she could hardly reach me as I tried to give her a kiss.

'Can I come in for a cup of tea?' I asked her.

'No,' she replied firmly. 'All my family are there.'

What I didn't realize then was that Karla is half-German and her family celebrated Christmas on 24th December; that night was their main celebration. There was a special family gathering in her house that evening which I mistakenly thought was the kind of drinking party that I loved. I was very glad later that I hadn't gone in because her Dad didn't approve of her bringing boys home, especially drunken ones. I could hardly stand and I would have made a complete fool of myself in front of Karla's parents.

'Can I see you again?' I asked.

'Phone me tomorrow,' she replied. 'You'll be sober then.' She seemed to have the measure of me, even then. I'm not sure she would have wanted to see me again though if she had realized that I had another three girl-friends on the go as well!

'Give your phone number to my brother,' I told her, 'I'll only lose it.'

The next day was Christmas Day, and I woke up at about eleven with a terrible hangover. As I lay in bed feeling dreadful, my brother handed me the slip of paper and told me that I had to ring the girl whose name was written on it. I groaned.

'What girl? What does she look like?'

'Just ring her Haydn!' He was fed up with my drunken exploits and didn't want to talk about it.

'I can't remember anything about her.' I said. 'I don't think I'll bother.'

When my Mam found out, she said, 'Haydn, you ought to ring her, if only out of courtesy.'

'OK, OK. What is it with you people? I'll give her a ring; when I've watched *Top of the Pops*.'

I wasn't going to miss the Christmas edition of *Top of the Pops* for anything. That year they had Olivia Newton-John singing 'You're the One that I want' from the film Grease; then there was ABBA, Kate Bush, Boney M, and even Father Abraham and the Smurfs!

After the show I went reluctantly over to the phone and dialled the numbers; I still didn't want to make the call.

'This is me, is that you?' I said. I wasn't at my best!

Fortunately it was her, and we arranged to meet that evening at seven. I was dreading it; I couldn't even remember what she looked like! What if I thought she was ugly? What if she didn't like me?

I drove up in the Cortina as arranged, and I saw a girl standing in the dim light from a shop window. I could see enough of her to make me decide not to drive straight past! I wound the window down.

'Are you Karla?'

'Yes, are you Haydn?'

As she climbed into the car, my first thoughts were: 'She's so short she can hardly see over the dashboard.' She was only five foot one.

'Wow, this is a posh car!' she said as she got in. She had expected me to arrive in an old banger.

We decided to go to the Vale of Glamorgan, a wealthy, farming area, and look for a good pub. But this was Christmas night, and so of course we couldn't find one that was open. Eventually we set off towards home, and found that the Fox and Hounds in Brynmenyn was open. As we entered the noisy, dimly-lit interior, I realized that a bunch of my mates from Bettws were there. They were drinking and there was plenty of banter.

'All right, boys?' I greeted them in the customary way. They looked Karla over as I led her to a table at the other side of the pub. I knew they were discussing my new girlfriend, and I longed to go over and be part of the fun. Instead, I had to be on my best behaviour, sitting and making polite conversation, and because I was driving I had to drink shandies. Christmas night and no drink! I was bored and fidgety, and I started to look over to where the lads were.

'You'd prefer to be over there with your mates, wouldn't you?' Karla said.

'No,' I replied unconvincingly.

At the end of the evening, I took her home and asked her if I could see her again. I was hoping that she would be eager for another date.

'Yes, but not too soon,' Karla replied coolly, 'I don't like getting involved.'

Her answer suited me, because I thought she wouldn't demand more commitment than I was ready to give. Still, it would have been better for my ego if she had been keener and as I drove away, I muttered to myself, 'I'll show her, that snooty little thing.' Karla had become a personal challenge.

We dated periodically after that. She told me that she had spent the previous Christmas in America with her sister and planned to go back, get a job and live there. We both accepted that our relationship would not be permanent.

'What are you doing at Whitsun? Do you fancy going somewhere together?' I asked once.

'No point,' she replied. 'We probably won't be together then.'

And I agreed with her, neither of us thought it would last.

On one occasion, we talked for a long time and I was able to explain to her all about my injuries and problems. I found Karla easy to talk to and shared with her things that I'd never told anyone. Although I wouldn't admit it, I was beginning to feel safe with her and I wanted to be with her. I realized that I didn't like the idea of her going out with someone else.

'I hope you don't two-time people,' I told her one day.

This was rich coming from me! Karla replied that she didn't do things like that and I knew that I could believe her. I still had three other girlfriends myself, but at the time my hypocritical attitude didn't bother me. Just because I was seeing other girls didn't mean that she could date other men.

Even though we both said we didn't want a commitment, we were becoming closer and more deeply involved with each other, more than we'd admit. One evening, when we had planned to go out together, I telephoned and told her that I'd decided to go with the boys instead.

'If that's how you feel, we may as well finish,' she said.

There was a long silence. I was taken aback because I thought she wouldn't mind.

'All right,' I said, and so it was her turn to be disappointed. We went on talking, both knowing that if we rang off it would be the end of our relationship. Eventually, we arranged to meet that night to 'say goodbye' to each other.

We sat in the pub miserable and in silence. Eventually both of us admitted that we wanted to continue the relationship. I had no interest any longer in the other girls that I was still dating. Karla had qualities I had not encountered in a woman before. On our first date, she had told me that she was twenty-seven. She was two and a half years older than me, far more mature, very strong-willed and able to put me in my place. I could talk to her about anything and we spent hours in conversation. She also had something very special that I sensed but did not yet understand. I wasn't only physically attracted to her. She had an inner beauty that intrigued me too.

Once, we wanted an evening alone together in the relaxed atmosphere of Bettws Club. A few tables away sat some friends with their partners.

'Come and join us,' they called. Easily led as I was, I would have done so, but Karla was firm.

'If you're too afraid to tell them you don't want to sit with them, tell them I don't want to be with them.'

She was strong and didn't care what anybody thought of her. I needed someone like that. She wouldn't be pushed around, and I liked that. There was one evening when we got back to my place after being down the pub, and my Dad was still up.

'She'll make us a cup of tea,' I told him.

'Who's she?' Karla replied dryly. I'd met my match.

The next day, my Dad said, 'That girl is fit for you, boy.' For my Dad to say that was a great compliment.

My relationship with Karla was deepening all the time. Every night, we spent hours on the telephone. We talked about whether her family would accept me, in my condition.

'I feel very self-conscious with your parents. How do they feel about their daughter having a relationship with a cripple?'

'Don't use that word,' she said. 'You need to respect yourself.'

'OK,' I replied. 'How do your parents feel about you having a relationship with a disabled person?'

'They are willing to accept anyone who makes me happy. Dad did warn me that there could be difficulties ahead, but he likes you.'

'I like them too. It feels as if I have another mother and father.'

Just then, Mam called along the hallway,

'Put that phone down, boy! You two monopolize that telephone for hours. Nobody else could get through if there was an emergency!'

'I'd better go,' I told Karla. 'Mam is getting mad.'

But we didn't ring off. We just couldn't spend enough time together. I didn't want to admit it, but I was in love with her.

Soon, I was spending every evening at Karla's house, often staying there until three, even though I knew I would have to get up early for work. The first person I thought about when I woke was Karla. I wished she were with me and not two miles away, but I felt very anxious about asking her to marry me. I didn't know how I would cope with the physical side of the relationship. Sometimes, I would lie awake in the night and think about how we would cope.

One day, Karla and I talked about marriage and I said, 'You wouldn't want to marry someone like me, would you?'

'Why not?'

'Well, you know,' I hesitated, 'I'm not sure how useful I'd be, you know, when we were together.'

'Haydn,' she said, 'I'd marry you even if we weren't able to have that kind of relationship.'

I was amazed at this answer and relieved. She accepted me for who I was, and it confirmed for me that she was the right person. This girl had said that she didn't mind if we never had sex. She would give up that whole aspect of a relationship just to be with me.

On 3rd March, 1979, we got engaged. We discussed a date for our wedding and at first we decided on July or August, when the factories were on holiday, especially as Karla's sister was coming over from America for a visit. However, once we felt that it was right to marry, we did not want to wait, and so we brought our wedding forward. I offered her a chapel wedding, but in the end we decided to have a quiet ceremony at Bridgend registry office. We laughed about the date. Karla had predicted that by Whitsun we were unlikely to be together, and yet here we were getting married.

14

BALL AND CHAIN

'What are you doing here?' I groaned, clutching my head and sinking back on my pillow as I woke up to Karla next to my bed.

'I've been here all night,' Karla told me. 'Your Mam insisted. The boys brought you home at about half-past eight, unconscious.'

Details of the night before came flooding back: my stag night! Waves of nausea swept over me. A night out with the lads was always a bad idea.

Mam put her head around the door.

'Oh, still alive, are you?' she asked, 'How are you feeling?'

'Terrible,' I croaked, trying not to move too suddenly. Mam gave me a fierce look.

'People have been known to choke on their own vomit when they have drunk as much as you did last night!' She pointed at Karla. 'This poor girl had to stay up with you. It's a good job you had your stag night a week before the wedding; it'll take the rest of the week for you to get over it!' Which of course was the whole idea, but I wasn't going to point that out then.

It always amazed me how confident and assertive Mam could be in her own home. When she went outside she was a different person: very nervous and quickly distressed. I realize now that she had her disabilities to cope with the same as I did; I just didn't realize it at the time. Because her illness wasn't physical it was harder to understand. And unlike mine she never really made any progress or recovery.

It took nearly the whole week for me to recover fully from the hangover; so that by Friday my head was clear and I had a chance to think about the enormity of what I would be doing the next day. I was getting married! This meant commitment. I started to panic.

'All this is happening too quickly,' I told myself, 'This is my last night as a single person!'

I didn't sleep well that night, and on the day itself I was sick with nerves. A pale, white face looked back at me as I checked myself in the bathroom mirror. I was thankful to see my best man, Peter, as he turned up to collect me. He was in a good mood.

'All right Haydn?'

'Yes fine thanks,' I said.

'You don't look well, you sure you're OK?'

'I'm OK. Come on let's go.'

We were driving to the registry office, and I was trying to keep my act together and be calm even though my stomach was in knots. I would have been feeling a lot better had Peter not decided that it would be really funny to rev the car so that it accelerated down the road, and then put his foot on the brake, bringing us almost to an emergency stop. He did this several times: stop, start; stop, start; chuckling to himself. The old Cortina jerked its way down the road.

'Give it a rest Peter!' My stomach, already delicate with the nerves, was all over the place and I was beginning to feel nauseous.

why did you say, 'Keep that frog away from me' as soon as you saw him?'

'I was hallucinating,' I replied defensively.

'Well, you are getting better now and you'll soon be up and about again.'

It was true; I was getting better.

We had arrived back to the bungalow as newly-weds, fully aware however that we would not have the privacy and space that we needed to accommodate our new life together. Before the wedding my parents and Alan had lived with me. However, we all knew that the bungalow had been given to me with certain rules and regulations: if I married or died, my parents had to be re-housed elsewhere.

This made things difficult and unpleasant for all of us; I felt as if I were throwing my parents out of their own home. While they were waiting to be re-housed, we all stayed together, with the inevitable tensions that this caused.

But when Mam, Dad and Alan finally left, I was apprehensive about them going. I wanted to make a home with my new wife, but I had depended on them for so long that it was hard to imagine life without their daily care. For a while, the bungalow was almost completely empty of furniture and didn't really feel like home. However with our combined incomes – Karla worked as a payroll clerk at the local factory – we could buy things quickly, and we enjoyed building up a home together. The first nice thing we bought was a display cabinet with glass doors. It gave Karla immense pleasure to fill it with pretty ornaments.

Soon after we were married, Karla and I visited Benny Jones, the former secretary of Lewistown AFC, to thank him for our wedding present. By this time he was in his seventies and bedridden because he had one of his legs amputated. We had managed to keep in touch; he had been devastated by the news of my accident, but pleased at the progress I was making. We both knew though that I would never play football again. As soon as we walked into the room, he pointed his finger towards me, and with tears in his eyes he said, 'You should've been in Arsenal, you should've been in Arsenal!' It was at moments like this that the hard facts sank in: I could have been a professional player but was now relegated to a life on the sidelines. There was nothing I could do to change this. Like Benny I had passed my best; the difference being that I was still in my twenties, he was in his seventies.

Still, I had the whole of my married life ahead. Newly wed I realized that it was time to settle down and I behaved myself fairly well at first. However, now twenty-six years old, I was not mature enough to keep it up. I still hankered after the freedom and fun I felt I had lost because of my years in hospital and I didn't want to think that the lads were having fun without me. Before too long, I began to feel trapped. It started with going out once a week with the boys, but soon developed into two or three times a week. Gradually, I slid further into my bad ways, drinking excessively and gambling until I was living like a single man again. Karla did her best to cope with it. She would try different tactics to get me to stay in with her. I knew she was good at darts, for example, and I was puzzled when I found out that she had packed the team in. I asked her about it.

'How come you're staying in on Tuesday nights, Karla? I thought you were playing darts.'

'I thought I'd do something different for a change,' my new wife replied, looking me straight in the eye.

'But isn't there a match every Tuesday? You're a good player; your team need you.'

'I thought I'd give it a rest for a while. Stay in with you. Now that we are married, we should go out together. I don't want to go out on my own and have you out with the boys.'

I knew what was on her mind. If she had an evening out, I'd use it as an excuse to have another night out with the boys and do even more drinking. Although Karla and I did go out together, I was showing signs of split loyalties.

Karla was completely committed to our marriage. However, on most weekends she hardly saw me because I was out with the boys; sometimes I didn't come home until four or five in the morning. As my behaviour deteriorated, we came close to separating.

Once I was out with my friends at the pub. 'Your wife is waiting for you at the door.' He added dryly, 'I suppose you'll have to go home now.'

'No way,' I protested, much too macho to tolerate the idea that I was under my wife's thumb. Reluctantly I added, 'I suppose I'd better see what she wants.'

Karla had walked for half a mile in the rain because I had forgotten to take my pills. I snatched the pills from her and went back into the pub with my mates and Karla walked off along the wet road to make the return journey. I knew that I was acting out of order and didn't deserve Karla, but I couldn't help myself. I was a big boy who needed to grow up.

My life was a cycle of working hard all week and drinking all weekend, constantly getting into trouble. In fact, I was deeply unhappy. I didn't know what I really wanted, whether to be married or single. I found it hard to adapt to the fact that I couldn't talk to other girls any more. I wasn't a womaniser, but I had spent years chatting up girls in clubs and I enjoyed doing it. I felt as if I had just regained my independence after the accident, and now I had lost it again through marriage.

Then in the midst of this turmoil Karla began to talk about having a baby.

Karla had always said that she wanted to have children, but I was far less keen, for a number of reasons. I thought I wouldn't be able to do ordinary, normal things for my child, even simple things like going for a walk; I was also scared that my children would be embarrassed by my disability and I didn't want them to be teased by others. However, I had a close friend who had lost a leg in a colliery accident. He had two little girls. I visited him one day and was deeply moved to see one of them kissing the stump that remained of his leg. I realized that, to them, he was normal, and I began to think that perhaps a child of mine could accept me as I was.

My greater, secret fear was that I'd lose more freedom. In some ways, I realized that having a family might be good. After all, many of my friends were fathers now. Deep inside, I knew that I needed to grow up and take responsibility, even if I was not willing to admit it. So I went along with Karla's wish.

We were not using contraception but Karla didn't become pregnant. Years before, my doctors had told me that it was highly unlikely that I would be able to father children but Karla was adamant that we would be OK. She felt a deep inner certainty that she could not explain.

One day when we travelled to Rookwood Hospital for my regular check-up, we met a new doctor, Dr Buni; he seemed to be kind and helpful and so we had a chat about it.

'Have you thought of having children?' he said.

'Not really,' I replied. 'I thought it would not be possible.'

'Well, there may be ways that we can help you, but we'll have to do some tests first.'

He recommended that I go to Heath Hospital in Cardiff – the same hospital I had been to earlier for an operation after the accident – to see a consultant called Mrs Sheila Walker. Karla and I both underwent tests to see whether we were able to have children. The results were promising but because of my spinal injuries, there were difficulties. The experts decided that we would use artificial insemination by husband (AIH), a relatively new technique in those days, and one that seemed far from straightforward.

I was expected to produce a sperm sample and race off to Heath Hospital with Karla so that she could be inseminated within two hours. The journey to Cardiff took nearly an hour and a half, and then we had to park the car and get to the right department in the huge hospital in time for it to be done. Talk about cutting it fine! The timing had to be right – Karla would have to take her temperature daily to know when she was ovulating. The whole thing was so unnatural and created so much anxiety that I found it impossible to relax and do my side of things.

We talked again to Mrs Walker and she suggested that the hospital should send us a 'home kit' that would arrive in the post. We waited several months, but nothing arrived; eventually we telephoned the hospital. They said that one had been sent to us but that they would send another. We never did find out what had happened to the first kit. Perhaps it went to Bettws in Newport instead of Bettws, Bridgend. If so, then someone in Newport must have had a bit of a surprise in the post one morning!

When the kit finally arrived, we unpacked it eagerly. It was an extremely strange looking little gadget, and we laughed when we saw it because it seemed impossible that it would work. With little hope that this thing could possibly work, we waited for the right time of the month to use it. As we followed the instructions, we lost even more confidence and in the end could only laugh help-lessly at the ludicrousness of what we were doing. What a waste of time! We followed the guidelines though, and Karla stayed in bed for half an hour afterwards and I went off to work feeling strangely depressed. I had warmed to the idea of having a baby of our own, but I couldn't believe that this would work.

Three weeks later, Karla did a home pregnancy test. We waited to see if a black circle appeared on the tester. To our amazement, a black ring began to appear almost straight away and we watched excitedly as it darkened. Karla was pregnant and later, this was confirmed by our doctor. It seemed a miracle that she had conceived at our first inept attempt at using this pathetic little tube!

We were overjoyed. I had told friends that I could not have children and when we announced our news, peo-ple were thrilled for us. We rang everyone we knew and told them. I was so pleased, but at the back of my mind I still had a nagging fear; given the extent of my injuries, would our child be normal?

For the first three months, Karla was so unwell that she had to stay in bed: she was sick, unable to eat, and liable to faint if she tried to walk around. After that, she bloomed and loved being pregnant. I was unable to enjoy this time as much as I would have liked, so obsessed was I about the baby's normality. However at the same time, I did spend the months dreaming about watching my son – and I was convinced that it would be a boy – play football. At last, another chance to relive my dream, or so I thought.

Towards the end of her pregnancy, Karla's blood pressure rose alarmingly and she was taken into hospital. No one had told us if we needed to tell the nurses that our child had been conceived by AIH. We weren't sure whether it would make any difference to Karla's treatment. Karla forgot the correct terminology and told the nurse, 'My baby was conceived though AID but my husband is the father. It wasn't a donor.'

The sister must have written AID (Artificial Insemination by Donor) on her notes by mistake, because when the duty doctor came to examine her, he asked her for the name of the father. She was very upset by his words; throughout the pregnancy she had been conscious that people might think that I could not be her baby's father. Little did she realize that when our beautiful baby daughter was born, she would look just like me!

Hayley's arrival proved to be a shock for all of us. It was our fourth wedding anniversary, and I was up at the hospital with Karla for her routine check-up.

'Your waters have broken, Mrs Davies,' said one of the nurses, 'we'll have to keep you in.'

What? But they can't have, it wasn't time. We weren't ready. We looked at each other, hands clasped, in disbelief. I panicked. They called for the doctor immediately.

'I'll just go home for my things,' Karla replied, but the doctor shook his head.

'Your husband will have to do it,' he told her. 'You'll have to stay here in case something happens on the way home.'

I rushed home to fetch Karla's suitcase, pleased to escape from the hospital. I'd had enough of them to last me a lifetime, and coming in with Karla had already proved to be a stressful time. About a month earlier, we had heard one of the other mother's screams as she struggled with her labour. I found this very hard to cope with;

all the memories of being in hospital, and the shouting and screaming I had experienced during my time at Cardiff and Rookwood came flooding back. In the end I panicked and staggered out of the place as fast as I could.

When I came back with Karla's case at about four that afternoon, she was in a room on her own and had been put on a drip because she was not having contractions. Nothing much had happened, and the crisis seemed to have passed. My mind turned to other matters.

'The FA Cup replay is on tonight,' I told her.

'You can go home and watch it, if you like,' she said. 'I'll ring you if anything happens.'

I made my escape, and Dad and I watched the match together. Dad was a great fan of Manchester United, and so we watched the game with excitement.

At half-time I telephoned the hospital to make enquiries about Karla. The nurse replied, 'Your wife and the baby are doing fine.'

'Baby?' I shouted.

'Yes,' said the nurse, 'Mrs Davies has had an emergency Caesarean, but she is doing well.'

Why didn't they phone me sooner? How had I missed my baby's arrival? 'Is it a boy or a girl?' I spluttered.

'Wouldn't you like to find that out when you come down here?' replied the nurse.

I used my best persuasive techniques and the nurse admitted that we had a lovely baby girl.

Dad and Mam were both in the sitting room; they had come to look after me while Karla was in hospital; I told them the news.

'You'll never believe this! We've had a girl.' I sounded disappointed, and in a way I was. A daughter wouldn't be able to become a top class football player. A stupid reaction I know, and one which was completely dispelled when I saw my daughter for the first time.

After the match Dad and I went to the hospital and he was given permission to come in with me, even though this was strictly against the rules. In fact, he saw her before Karla did, because Hayley was taken straight into the special care unit to be checked. He was thrilled to be a grandad.

As soon as I saw my baby daughter, I fell in love with her. She was lovely, with long limbs and perfect features. Karla and I had already chosen a name for her and I murmured it to myself: 'Lydia.'

'She's exactly like you,' said the nurse.

'Thanks,' I replied, feeling relieved that no one could be in any doubt that I really was her father.

Karla was still fast asleep from the anaesthetic so Dad and I decided to go home. Later that evening, the two of us watched a film starring Hayley Mills.

'That's a nice name, boy,' he said.

'I like it, too. It would be a pretty name for my daughter.' I tried it out a few times.

'Yes. All I have to do now is convince Karla!'

I visited Karla next day to find her exhausted but on an emotional high. Still affected by the anaesthetic, she was not really capable of making a decision. Still, I put the idea to her and she agreed, although I don't think she knew what it was that she was agreeing to.

Karla had to stay in hospital for the next ten days. We were deeply grateful to the medical staff; they made sure that Karla had the best care. I visited every day, longing to have my wife and baby home with me.

When the day finally came for them to come home, a nurse carried Hayley to the car and placed her in Karla's arms. At that moment I really felt like a husband and a Dad, and I was proud to introduce little Hayley to my Mam. She had been unable to visit the hospital, and so it was a special moment when she was able to hold her grandchild for the first time.

'It's like holding you all over again, Haydn,' she said tearfully.

Mam and Dad stayed for a week to help Karla adjust. Grateful though we were, we couldn't wait to be alone with our tiny daughter. I would drive home from work each day full of excitement to see her.

Reality soon hit me though. You can't go out whenever you like and you have to take such a lot with you when you do manage to venture out.

For a few months, I enjoyed the novelty of fatherhood, although there were big adjustments for both of us. We soon found out how drastically life changes with the arrival of a baby. Everything takes much longer than it used to, and you have to start planning for things in advance. On top of this, Hayley suffered from night colic and we had plenty of sleepless nights.

I became restless, and started drifting into my old habits, and it didn't take long for me to get back in with the lads. Usually I was first into the pub and last out – and after that I would go on to parties or get food from the local Indian and Chinese restaurants. As before, I often did not arrive home until four or five in the morning. Karla was angry and disappointed. She knew that it was pointless to argue with me when I was drunk, but next day she would tell me exactly what she thought of me. I didn't really care enough to listen to what she said.

'If you don't like it, you can clear off!' I told her.

The truth was that I placed a low value on marriage, and sometimes I did feel like leaving. The major thing that stopped me from leaving was the fear that I wouldn't be able to see Hayley. In her desperate attempts to get me to behave more responsibly, Karla had threatened that if we split up, she would not let me have contact with our baby.

Things came to a head one evening when Hayley was three years old. I staggered home from a works party, noisy, argumentative and extremely drunk, eventually falling flat on the floor and unable to get up.

'Leave me alone,' I shouted repeatedly as Karla tried to get me to my feet and put me to bed. Hayley came from her bedroom, frightened and puzzled.

'What's the matter with Daddy?' she asked, obviously upset, thinking that I had fallen and hurt myself. It suddenly hit me. I was doing this to her! She was now old enough to see me drunk and work out that something was wrong. In fact, because I had come home relatively early, this was the first time that Hayley had seen me in this state, and even in my drunkenness I could sense her fear and confusion. I was so ashamed of what I had done.

For the first time I really understood what the drink was doing to me, to Karla, and now also to Hayley. I vowed that it would be the last time. Surely this had been my wake-up call.

15

THE ANSWER TO EVERYTHING

'I know I've got to get my act together,' I admitted to
Karla. 'I'm like a hamster on a wheel; caught in a vicious
circle of working all week and being drunk all weekend.
There has to be more to life than this.'

'You've said that before,' replied Karla sceptically.
'Nothing ever changes.'

'Yes, but I'm older now.' I struggled to express what I
was feeling. 'I'm still behaving like a teenager. I've got a
really good wife, a lovely daughter and all the material
things I could want, but my life is still empty.' It was
such a relief to admit this to her. I had been putting on a
front for so long: acting like I was OK, and pretending
everything was all right, when I knew it wasn't. In a way
I'd been doing this ever since the accident, but I didn't
want to pretend any more.

'The only way things are going to change will be if
you stop drinking,' she told me. Then she added,
'Maybe it would help if we tried going to church.'

'Church?' I exclaimed.

Church was the last thing I had in mind! I used to get
thrown out of RE at school. I hated everything to do with
religion: I didn't like hymns, and I didn't understand all

of the religious language they used. To me, church was outdated and irrelevant. I wasn't at all interested in any of that. Karla had made this suggestion before but I had always refused bluntly. 'What good would church be?' I had often replied. But she had often brought it up.

When I first met Karla I knew that there was something different about her, but I didn't know what. I didn't know that she was a Christian who had left the church. Gradually I got to know her story. A committed Christian until the age of twenty-one, Karla had gone through a personal crisis and decided that she wanted to see what it was like to live a different way. Almost from the day of our marriage, she'd wanted to return to her faith and to church. And now she was suggesting that this might be the answer to my crisis too!

'I don't mind you going to church if you want to,' I said, 'but you'll have to go on your own, and don't ask me to come with you again.'

But Karla didn't want to go on her own. She was afraid that it would give me an excuse for still more nights out with the boys. Deep down, I began to think that perhaps she was right about church. I also began to wonder whether it was Karla's faith that had carried her through our first few years of marriage.

One day I finally gave in.

'I may as well give it a go. My life is in such a mess that I have nothing to lose. Anyway, for years you've gone everywhere I wanted to go. I owe it to you to go somewhere you want to go, for once.'

This was quite a turnaround for me to actually admit what we both knew to be true. Karla jumped at the chance.

'That's great,' Karla replied, carefully masking her excitement. 'How about next Sunday evening?'

'OK,' I agreed. I was nervous of course, but too macho to admit it. Karla continued. She explained that I couldn't judge a church by this one service and asked if I would attend for a month to give it a fair trial. Reluctantly, I agreed.

So this was it. Haydn Davies agreeing to go to church! I definitely wasn't going to tell my friends. It was all right in the valleys for a girl to go to church – she was a lovely person – but a man – he would be considered a sissy. No, this was going to be something I kept tight-lipped about. Nevertheless, I kept my word.

When we arrived at the local evangelical church, Calfaria Baptist, those people who knew Karla were delighted to see her again and they gave us both a big welcome. One lady, known to everyone as Auntie Syb, said that she had been praying for this day for many years. Apparently she had been praying for me as well as for Karla. I took this with a pinch of salt. How could this lady be praying for me when she didn't know me?

Throughout the service, I felt extremely bored and couldn't wait to get out. An enormously tall man stood at the door, greeting everyone as they left. Although I did not realize it, he was the minister, Reverend David Carey-Jones. He was about six foot five and had a deep voice. He shook my hand and asked me a few questions about myself. I looked up at this gentle giant and thought he must be God. But I still couldn't wait to get out; we were going on to the local disco after church.

'Who is this "Amazing Grace" lady then?' I asked as we got into the car. 'They didn't half go on about her.'

Karla laughed as she explained that 'Amazing Grace' was one of the hymns that we had been singing.

Another week, two men came around with a small piece of bread and a little glass of red liquid.

'What a crabby lot!' I thought. 'They don't give you much to eat!'

Karla whispered, 'You can't have any. Just let it go past.'

'What an insult! They won't even share a bit of bread!' I thought. I didn't want any, anyway. It wasn't enough to feed a sparrow! When we were home, Karla explained that this was all part of communion, and that you could only take it if you were a Christian.

As we went each week, I noticed more and more. There was an old man who would sit at the front; his name was Tom Davies. All through the service he'd be shouting 'Amen!' I felt thoroughly annoyed with him because I thought it was rude. At least I was quiet.

'Stupid old man!' I thought. 'Why doesn't he shut up?'

Later, I discovered that Tom Davies was one of the greatest and godliest men you could ever meet.

I thought the most bizarre people went to this church. There was the man who gave out the books at the door – he frightened me to death. He was about eighty years old, deaf and had one eye. His good eye stared and watered incessantly while the other was permanently closed. Because of his deafness, he spoke strangely. He also had hair growing out of his ears. I used to send Karla in first to get the hymn books! She knew his background; he was actually a sweet-natured and lovely man, who, with his wife had been attending the church for about sixty years.

I was a man of my word and I went to church for a month. It felt like a prison sentence: I had done my time and I certainly did not expect to go back. Shortly after this I had to go into hospital yet again for an operation on my right knee. I was there for about a week before coming home to convalesce.

While I was at home recovering I had a visitor. Karla showed him in and I saw that it was the six foot five giant I had met at church. I wasn't sure who he was, so I called him the Vicar Man. Karla had tried to explain that he was the pastor, but to me pasta was a plate of food. I couldn't understand all of this strange terminology. Pastor Carey-Jones stayed for about half an hour and seemed interested in me and how I was doing.

After he left, I told Karla 'It was really nice of that Vicar Man to come and visit.' Then after a moment more I continued, 'Just to repay him for his kindness, and to thank God for my beautiful little daughter, I will be really good and go to church once more.'

I had to wait two months until my leg was out of plaster before I could keep my word, and by that time it was late autumn in 1985. This was going to be the last time I went, and I didn't want Karla to be under any illusions. I still thought it was boring, but for some reason, after the service I found myself telling Karla, 'I'm going to be really, really good to you now and stay until Christmas. Then I'm off! No more after that!'

This would compensate for all that I had put her through. During this time I stopped resisting church and got on with my stint of attendance.

'While I'm here,' I thought, 'I might as well try to listen.' But it was still all Double Dutch to me. I noticed that most other people were listening intently and enjoying the service. Why were they finding it so exciting when I was so bored? What was I missing?

After church one evening, an old lady called Mrs Gough asked whether I wanted to come to a fellowship meeting one Saturday evening. I still didn't know why they used all these strange terms, and I didn't know what she meant. I said I'd go along anyway though, to see what it was like. Then it suddenly dawned upon me. Saturday night after the match was of course when the boys would be going out to have a good time. Here I was going to a fellowship meeting! But I said I would go, and I intended to keep to my word.

We went along and Mrs Gough let us in. The place was full of old people, and nearly all women, too. I sat next to Auntie Syb, who I recognized as the church organist. The more I chatted to her, the more I liked her and wanted to learn from her. I came to realize that these religious people were normal people who loved God. However I was convinced that I would never be like them, I was so different. And, as I kept reminding myself, this was Saturday night . . .

'There is no way I'm staying here all night,' I promised myself. 'I'll stay for about an hour and then shoot off down the pub.'

I thought that nobody would miss me. But to my utter amazement, whenever I tried to get up and leave, I found that I was unable to move. It wasn't just that I was being lazy, or that my legs were stiff, I really could not move.

At around 10:30 I tried again.

'I'll be off now and catch last orders,' I thought, but still I couldn't get up. What was it that was stopping me from going?

We stayed there until two in the morning and in the end there was just Karla, me, and Mrs Gough. We heard all about her life. She'd become a Christian not long after her marriage and for 45 years, she had prayed for her husband to become one too. He worked in the colliery and was as tough and as hardened as any of the men that went down the pit. She kept praying for him over all those years and then he had an amazing conversion experience and there was a dramatic change in his life. I did wonder what she meant by conversion experience but continued to listen. For the final five years of their marriage she said they were able to share their faith together.

'Our first prayer together was sweeter than our first kiss,' said Mrs Gough.

'Really?' I thought, 'How could that work?' I didn't say anything though.

As we were leaving the house in the early hours of the morning she said, 'Haydn, make sure you put yourself right with God, because he has brought you out of that car crash for a reason.'

Now this really touched me. What did she mean 'right with God'? How could she talk about the car crash like that? I had always wondered why I had survived when the others were killed and now I could not stop thinking about the old lady's words. Why had I stayed at her house until two in the morning? What had kept me there? Was it the fact that these people were so different from me, that they had something that I had not yet experienced? As we left, I asked Karla to explain more to me about the Christian life.

We sat up talking for most of the rest of the night. Karla explained many things about Christianity to me. I tried to grasp them, but couldn't: salvation, repentance, forgiveness, why did there have to be such big words? I struggled to get my head round them all. Karla told me somewhere in the conversation that God could break down the resistance of the hardest heart. I beat my fist on my chest. 'There is no way He is going to break this heart.' I was not a bitter person, but had become very toughened as a result all the horrific things that I had been through and seen in hospital. I didn't fear anyone, even God.

The next day we went to church in the evening as usual. As I listened to the preacher, I felt uncomfortable, and squirmed in my seat. I wondered why this preacher was looking at me all the time, and how he knew so much about me. Had someone told him? He was saying things that I thought somebody must have told him about my life. I now know that it was the Holy Spirit, convicting me of my sins, and speaking directly to me.

I realized that Jesus Christ was speaking to me. He knew about me, knew what I had done, knew what I thought; He knew everything. I believe He was saying 'Haydn Davies, you carry your cross and follow me.' I had fought hard against it, with all my pride and determination, but something in my heart wanted to respond now; to sincerely say sorry for all the wrong things I had done. I knew then that I wanted to follow Jesus. And so this is what I did, I prayed for the first time. 'Lord Jesus, I know that I am a sinner. Please forgive me for my sins. Please make me into a new person like you say you will. Amen.' Immediately I felt peace inside, I felt clean.

I realized then that God had broken my hard resistant heart. I was a new person. No one told me this; I just knew that I was changed inside.

After the service, when I told the others what I'd prayed, they hugged and kissed me. This was too much and made me very uncomfortable. I didn't understand why they were making such a fuss. However, when Karla and I got home, she explained to me the importance of what I'd done.

'You've been saved, Haydn. Without Jesus, you would have gone to hell, but now you have a place in heaven. You have become a Christian. You remember we talked about this before. God has changed you.'

It was true. In October 1985 in Calfaria Baptist church, I repented of my sin and committed my life to Jesus. He was now my Lord and my Saviour. If someone had told me that they had done this and that they now felt peace, contentment and joy, I would have laughed at them. However I realized that only God could change people, and only God could change me. And this is how I felt – content and at peace. I just knew that my life had changed.

A NEW WAY OF LIVING

Had I really been saved? Could it be that God had forgiven my sins? Or was yesterday a dream? I woke up excited but unsure. Of course it had happened and I did feel like a burden had been lifted. Karla smiled when I told her how I felt.

'You've made a big decision and commitment, but it's the best decision that you could ever make.'

I knew it was. And I knew my life would have to change. I soon found solid evidence that what had happened to me was real and lasting. I used to swear a lot, being an ex-footballer and a factory worker. Now, every time I tried to swear, nothing would come out!

I carried on going to church every Sunday and started attending the prayer meeting on Tuesdays. Although I was still going to the pubs and clubs, gradually I felt less happy there and I felt like I didn't belong. I was more at home with the Christians; the danger was however that I thought I was a really good Christian, attending church and prayer meeting. It was almost as if I were doing God a favour. I still had a lot to learn about my new faith.

Karla and I began to pray together every night, an exciting new experience for me. I wanted so much to sober, I would not remember who she was; I'd even struggle to remember her name.

This was my life, for about two years: light duties at Christie-Tyler, lots of drinking, lots of chatting up girls and no commitments; and that suited me just fine. I had no desire to change the way I lived, or the way I treated girls; I was one of the lads.

It was Christmas Eve, 1978, and I was at the local disco as usual. As I walked in a girl called Pat, who I knew quite well, called out to me.

'Come and have a dance with me.'

'Later,' I replied. I was still sober and I needed a few drinks to dull my senses and build up the courage to dance. I spent the evening doing what I did best – joking with the lads and drinking. Just before the end of the night I remembered Pat and staggered over to where she had been sitting. She wasn't there any longer, but her friend was.

'Tell Pat I kept my promise,' I said to this girl, 'I came over to dance with her.'

'If you can dance with her, why can't you dance with me?' she asked, smiling.

So I did. I discovered that her name was Karla, and she discovered that I was so drunk I would fall over if she didn't hold on to me. I had seen her before and thought she was about eighteen, far too young for me; I was twenty-four. I was sober enough to notice that she was curvaceous, with dark hair and beautiful large brown eyes.

'When she's a bit older and has lost her puppy fat, she'll be a really lovely girl,' I thought, much to my dismay now. Because she had asked me to dance, I decided that she must be interested in me. With my usual bravado I tried my favourite chat-up line: 'Get your coat, I'm taking you home.'

'You can't take me home,' she replied. 'You're too drunk to drive, and anyway, I've already arranged to share a taxi with some friends.'

'I have a car waiting outside,' I said, knowing that as usual my brother was waiting to chauffeur me home. Karla looked at me dubiously. She was not very keen on the idea of going home with a drunk, chaperoned by his brother. I was persistent, though, and she gave in.

When we arrived at her home, I followed her out of the car. She was so tiny that, even standing on the kerb, she could hardly reach me as I tried to give her a kiss.

'Can I come in for a cup of tea?' I asked her.

'No,' she replied firmly. 'All my family are there.'

What I didn't realize then was that Karla is half-German and her family celebrated Christmas on 24th December; that night was their main celebration. There was a special family gathering in her house that evening which I mistakenly thought was the kind of drinking party that I loved. I was very glad later that I hadn't gone in because her Dad didn't approve of her bringing boys home, especially drunken ones. I could hardly stand and I would have made a complete fool of myself in front of Karla's parents.

'Can I see you again?' I asked.

'Phone me tomorrow,' she replied. 'You'll be sober then.' She seemed to have the measure of me, even then. I'm not sure she would have wanted to see me again though if she had realized that I had another three girl-friends on the go as well!

'Give your phone number to my brother,' I told her, 'I'll only lose it.'

The next day was Christmas Day, and I woke up at about eleven with a terrible hangover. As I lay in bed feeling dreadful, my brother handed me the slip of paper and told me that I had to ring the girl whose name was written on it. I groaned.

'What girl? What does she look like?'

'Just ring her Haydn!' He was fed up with my drunken exploits and didn't want to talk about it.

'I can't remember anything about her.' I said. 'I don't think I'll bother.'

When my Mam found out, she said, 'Haydn, you ought to ring her, if only out of courtesy.'

'OK, OK. What is it with you people? I'll give her a ring; when I've watched *Top of the Pops*.'

I wasn't going to miss the Christmas edition of *Top of the Pops* for anything. That year they had Olivia Newton-John singing 'You're the One that I want' from the film Grease; then there was ABBA, Kate Bush, Boney M, and even Father Abraham and the Smurfs!

After the show I went reluctantly over to the phone and dialled the numbers; I still didn't want to make the call.

'This is me, is that you?' I said. I wasn't at my best!

Fortunately it was her, and we arranged to meet that evening at seven. I was dreading it; I couldn't even remember what she looked like! What if I thought she was ugly? What if she didn't like me?

I drove up in the Cortina as arranged, and I saw a girl standing in the dim light from a shop window. I could see enough of her to make me decide not to drive straight past! I wound the window down.

'Are you Karla?'

'Yes, are you Haydn?'

As she climbed into the car, my first thoughts were: 'She's so short she can hardly see over the dashboard.' She was only five foot one.

'Wow, this is a posh car!' she said as she got in. She had expected me to arrive in an old banger.

We decided to go to the Vale of Glamorgan, a wealthy, farming area, and look for a good pub. But this was Christmas night, and so of course we couldn't find one that was open. Eventually we set off towards home, and found that the Fox and Hounds in Brynmenyn was open. As we entered the noisy, dimly-lit interior, I realized that a bunch of my mates from Bettws were there. They were drinking and there was plenty of banter.

'All right, boys?' I greeted them in the customary way. They looked Karla over as I led her to a table at the other side of the pub. I knew they were discussing my new girlfriend, and I longed to go over and be part of the fun. Instead, I had to be on my best behaviour, sitting and making polite conversation, and because I was driving I had to drink shandies. Christmas night and no drink! I was bored and fidgety, and I started to look over to where the lads were.

'You'd prefer to be over there with your mates, wouldn't you?' Karla said.

'No,' I replied unconvincingly.

At the end of the evening, I took her home and asked her if I could see her again. I was hoping that she would be eager for another date.

'Yes, but not too soon,' Karla replied coolly, 'I don't like getting involved.'

Her answer suited me, because I thought she wouldn't demand more commitment than I was ready to give. Still, it would have been better for my ego if she had been keener and as I drove away, I muttered to myself, 'I'll show her, that snooty little thing.' Karla had become a personal challenge.

We dated periodically after that. She told me that she had spent the previous Christmas in America with her sister and planned to go back, get a job and live there. We both accepted that our relationship would not be permanent.

'What are you doing at Whitsun? Do you fancy going somewhere together?' I asked once.

'No point,' she replied. 'We probably won't be together then.'

And I agreed with her, neither of us thought it would last.

On one occasion, we talked for a long time and I was able to explain to her all about my injuries and problems. I found Karla easy to talk to and shared with her things that I'd never told anyone. Although I wouldn't admit it, I was beginning to feel safe with her and I wanted to be with her. I realized that I didn't like the idea of her going out with someone else.

'I hope you don't two-time people,' I told her one day.

This was rich coming from me! Karla replied that she didn't do things like that and I knew that I could believe her. I still had three other girlfriends myself, but at the time my hypocritical attitude didn't bother me. Just because I was seeing other girls didn't mean that she could date other men.

Even though we both said we didn't want a commitment, we were becoming closer and more deeply involved with each other, more than we'd admit. One evening, when we had planned to go out together, I telephoned and told her that I'd decided to go with the boys instead.

'If that's how you feel, we may as well finish,' she said.

There was a long silence. I was taken aback because I thought she wouldn't mind.

'All right,' I said, and so it was her turn to be disappointed. We went on talking, both knowing that if we rang off it would be the end of our relationship. Eventually, we arranged to meet that night to 'say goodbye' to each other.

We sat in the pub miserable and in silence. Eventually both of us admitted that we wanted to continue the relationship. I had no interest any longer in the other girls that I was still dating. Karla had qualities I had not encountered in a woman before. On our first date, she had told me that she was twenty-seven. She was two and a half years older than me, far more mature, very strong-willed and able to put me in my place. I could talk to her about anything and we spent hours in conversation. She also had something very special that I sensed but did not yet understand. I wasn't only physically attracted to her. She had an inner beauty that intrigued me too.

Once, we wanted an evening alone together in the relaxed atmosphere of Bettws Club. A few tables away sat some friends with their partners.

'Come and join us,' they called. Easily led as I was, I would have done so, but Karla was firm.

'If you're too afraid to tell them you don't want to sit with them, tell them I don't want to be with them.'

She was strong and didn't care what anybody thought of her. I needed someone like that. She wouldn't be pushed around, and I liked that. There was one evening when we got back to my place after being down the pub, and my Dad was still up.

'She'll make us a cup of tea,' I told him.

'Who's she?' Karla replied dryly. I'd met my match.

The next day, my Dad said, 'That girl is fit for you, boy.' For my Dad to say that was a great compliment.

My relationship with Karla was deepening all the time. Every night, we spent hours on the telephone. We talked about whether her family would accept me, in my condition.

'I feel very self-conscious with your parents. How do they feel about their daughter having a relationship with a cripple?'

'Don't use that word,' she said. 'You need to respect yourself.'

'OK,' I replied. 'How do your parents feel about you having a relationship with a disabled person?'

'They are willing to accept anyone who makes me happy. Dad did warn me that there could be difficulties ahead, but he likes you.'

'I like them too. It feels as if I have another mother and father.'

Just then, Mam called along the hallway,

'Put that phone down, boy! You two monopolize that telephone for hours. Nobody else could get through if there was an emergency!'

'I'd better go,' I told Karla. 'Mam is getting mad.'

But we didn't ring off. We just couldn't spend enough time together. I didn't want to admit it, but I was in love with her.

Soon, I was spending every evening at Karla's house, often staying there until three, even though I knew I would have to get up early for work. The first person I thought about when I woke was Karla. I wished she were with me and not two miles away, but I felt very anxious about asking her to marry me. I didn't know how I would cope with the physical side of the relationship. Sometimes, I would lie awake in the night and think about how we would cope.

One day, Karla and I talked about marriage and I said, 'You wouldn't want to marry someone like me, would you?'

'Why not?'

'Well, you know,' I hesitated, 'I'm not sure how useful I'd be, you know, when we were together.'

'Haydn,' she said, 'I'd marry you even if we weren't able to have that kind of relationship.'

I was amazed at this answer and relieved. She accepted me for who I was, and it confirmed for me that she was the right person. This girl had said that she didn't mind if we never had sex. She would give up that whole aspect of a relationship just to be with me.

On 3rd March, 1979, we got engaged. We discussed a date for our wedding and at first we decided on July or August, when the factories were on holiday, especially as Karla's sister was coming over from America for a visit. However, once we felt that it was right to marry, we did not want to wait, and so we brought our wedding forward. I offered her a chapel wedding, but in the end we decided to have a quiet ceremony at Bridgend registry office. We laughed about the date. Karla had predicted that by Whitsun we were unlikely to be together, and yet here we were getting married.

BALL AND CHAIN

'What are you doing here?' I groaned, clutching my head and sinking back on my pillow as I woke up to Karla next to my bed.

'I've been here all night,' Karla told me. 'Your Mam insisted. The boys brought you home at about half-past eight, unconscious.'

Details of the night before came flooding back: my stag night! Waves of nausea swept over me. A night out with the lads was always a bad idea.

Mam put her head around the door.

'Oh, still alive, are you?' she asked, 'How are you feeling?'

'Terrible,' I croaked, trying not to move too suddenly. Mam gave me a fierce look.

'People have been known to choke on their own vomit when they have drunk as much as you did last night!' She pointed at Karla. 'This poor girl had to stay up with you. It's a good job you had your stag night a week before the wedding; it'll take the rest of the week for you to get over it!' Which of course was the whole idea, but I wasn't going to point that out then.

It always amazed me how confident and assertive Mam could be in her own home. When she went outside she was a different person: very nervous and quickly distressed. I realize now that she had her disabilities to cope with the same as I did; I just didn't realize it at the time. Because her illness wasn't physical it was harder to understand. And unlike mine she never really made any progress or recovery.

It took nearly the whole week for me to recover fully from the hangover; so that by Friday my head was clear and I had a chance to think about the enormity of what I would be doing the next day. I was getting married! This meant commitment. I started to panic.

'All this is happening too quickly,' I told myself, 'This is my last night as a single person!'

I didn't sleep well that night, and on the day itself I was sick with nerves. A pale, white face looked back at me as I checked myself in the bathroom mirror. I was thankful to see my best man, Peter, as he turned up to collect me. He was in a good mood.

'All right Haydn?'

'Yes fine thanks,' I said.

'You don't look well, you sure you're OK?'

'I'm OK. Come on let's go.'

We were driving to the registry office, and I was trying to keep my act together and be calm even though my stomach was in knots. I would have been feeling a lot better had Peter not decided that it would be really funny to rev the car so that it accelerated down the road, and then put his foot on the brake, bringing us almost to an emergency stop. He did this several times: stop, start; stop, start; chuckling to himself. The old Cortina jerked its way down the road.

'Give it a rest Peter!' My stomach, already delicate with the nerves, was all over the place and I was beginning to feel nauseous.

Eventually we arrived. I stopped in my tracks as I saw standing at the front of the registry office one of my old girlfriends staring straight at me! What was she doing here? This was the last thing I needed. I tried to ignore her, but she wasn't having any of that and she came up and gave me a big kiss right in front of Karla, who didn't even know who she was.

I don't remember much about the day itself. I was nervous, tired, and probably still affected by the alcohol from the stag night. I think that we were both relieved when the day was over, looking forward to some time away. However, the honeymoon was brief and not what we hoped for. It turned out I was ill, I had a chest infection which got so bad over the next couple of days that we had to come home early.

After we got back we were able to remember more of the day itself as we sat down to look at some of the wedding photos.

'Crikey!' Karla exclaimed. 'My mum's managed to cut off the top of almost every person's head. What a pity she insisted on taking the photographs – there's not much here that we can frame and put on show.'

I picked up a picture of myself arriving at the registry office with my best man Peter as my chauffeur. Karla laughed.

'You looked pretty bleary-eyed!'

'I had not slept much!' I retorted. 'I was sick with nerves.'

'And who was that girl standing by the registry office door?' Karla asked. 'The one you said you didn't know – just before she gave you a big kiss.'

'Well, it was one of my ex-girlfriends,' I admitted, 'I didn't know she was going to be there. She was the last person I wanted to see. I expect Mam told her I was getting married.'

I didn't know how my new wife would react to this; Karla laughed it off, thank goodness.

The next picture was of Karla and me emerging from the ceremony, looking very happy. The day itself had been a whirlwind of movement. Perhaps for the first time I remember feeling intensely relieved and glad I had gone through with it.

'Here's one at our reception,' said Karla, holding out a photograph of us sitting in her parent's front parlour. 'Look at your Mam, all dressed up to the nines even though she couldn't manage it to the ceremony. She looks so proud of you.'

'She had a really good time. We all did,' I said.

'And here's one of the car, all tied up with old boots and sprayed with shaving foam. We had to stop at the first lay-by and clean it. Pity it broke down on the way. We only had to go forty miles.'

'Mmm,' I replied. 'The whole thing was a disaster, really.'

'Oh, no,' Karla said firmly. 'The Gower is beautiful and it was a great hotel, even if we did have to struggle there in third gear after the automatic gearbox broke down.' We laughed. She held up a photograph of one of the glorious views of mountain and coastline that make the Gower landscapes famous.

I picked up a picture of myself sitting near the hotel pool. I looked pretty ill, although I was smiling and trying to hide it.

'I thought I was going to be one of the few people who actually die on their honeymoon,' I said.

'You couldn't help being ill and I didn't mind coming home early.'

'Well, I'm sorry it happened.'

'Of course you were. That doctor we called said it was a really severe asthma attack.' She laughed again. 'But why did you say, 'Keep that frog away from me' as soon as you saw him?'

'I was hallucinating,' I replied defensively.

'Well, you are getting better now and you'll soon be up and about again.'

It was true; I was getting better.

We had arrived back to the bungalow as newly-weds, fully aware however that we would not have the privacy and space that we needed to accommodate our new life together. Before the wedding my parents and Alan had lived with me. However, we all knew that the bungalow had been given to me with certain rules and regulations: if I married or died, my parents had to be re-housed elsewhere.

This made things difficult and unpleasant for all of us; I felt as if I were throwing my parents out of their own home. While they were waiting to be re-housed, we all stayed together, with the inevitable tensions that this caused.

But when Mam, Dad and Alan finally left, I was apprehensive about them going. I wanted to make a home with my new wife, but I had depended on them for so long that it was hard to imagine life without their daily care. For a while, the bungalow was almost completely empty of furniture and didn't really feel like home. However with our combined incomes – Karla worked as a payroll clerk at the local factory – we could buy things quickly, and we enjoyed building up a home together. The first nice thing we bought was a display cabinet with glass doors. It gave Karla immense pleasure to fill it with pretty ornaments.

Soon after we were married, Karla and I visited Benny Jones, the former secretary of Lewistown AFC, to thank him for our wedding present. By this time he was in his seventies and bedridden because he had one of his legs amputated. We had managed to keep in touch; he had been devastated by the news of my accident, but pleased at the progress I was making. We both knew though that I would never play football again. As soon as we walked into the room, he pointed his finger towards me, and with tears in his eyes he said, 'You should've been in Arsenal, you should've been in Arsenal!' It was at moments like this that the hard facts sank in: I could have been a professional player but was now relegated to a life on the sidelines. There was nothing I could do to change this. Like Benny I had passed my best; the difference being that I was still in my twenties, he was in his seventies.

Still, I had the whole of my married life ahead. Newly wed I realized that it was time to settle down and I behaved myself fairly well at first. However, now twenty-six years old, I was not mature enough to keep it up. I still hankered after the freedom and fun I felt I had lost because of my years in hospital and I didn't want to think that the lads were having fun without me. Before too long, I began to feel trapped. It started with going out once a week with the boys, but soon developed into two or three times a week. Gradually, I slid further into my bad ways, drinking excessively and gambling until I was living like a single man again. Karla did her best to cope with it. She would try different tactics to get me to stay in with her. I knew she was good at darts, for example, and I was puzzled when I found out that she had packed the team in. I asked her about it.

'How come you're staying in on Tuesday nights, Karla? I thought you were playing darts.'

'I thought I'd do something different for a change,' my new wife replied, looking me straight in the eye.

'But isn't there a match every Tuesday? You're a good player; your team need you.'

'I thought I'd give it a rest for a while. Stay in with you. Now that we are married, we should go out together. I don't want to go out on my own and have you out with the boys.'

I knew what was on her mind. If she had an evening out, I'd use it as an excuse to have another night out with the boys and do even more drinking. Although Karla and I did go out together, I was showing signs of split loyalties.

Karla was completely committed to our marriage. However, on most weekends she hardly saw me because I was out with the boys; sometimes I didn't come home until four or five in the morning. As my behaviour deteriorated, we came close to separating.

Once I was out with my friends at the pub. 'Your wife is waiting for you at the door.' He added dryly, 'I suppose you'll have to go home now.'

'No way,' I protested, much too macho to tolerate the idea that I was under my wife's thumb. Reluctantly I added, 'I suppose I'd better see what she wants.'

Karla had walked for half a mile in the rain because I had forgotten to take my pills. I snatched the pills from her and went back into the pub with my mates and Karla walked off along the wet road to make the return journey. I knew that I was acting out of order and didn't deserve Karla, but I couldn't help myself. I was a big boy who needed to grow up.

My life was a cycle of working hard all week and drinking all weekend, constantly getting into trouble. In fact, I was deeply unhappy. I didn't know what I really wanted, whether to be married or single. I found it hard to adapt to the fact that I couldn't talk to other girls any more. I wasn't a womaniser, but I had spent years chatting up girls in clubs and I enjoyed doing it. I felt as if I had just regained my independence after the accident, and now I had lost it again through marriage.

Then in the midst of this turmoil Karla began to talk about having a baby.

Karla had always said that she wanted to have children, but I was far less keen, for a number of reasons. I thought I wouldn't be able to do ordinary, normal things for my child, even simple things like going for a walk; I was also scared that my children would be embarrassed by my disability and I didn't want them to be teased by others. However, I had a close friend who had lost a leg in a colliery accident. He had two little girls. I visited him one day and was deeply moved to see one of them kissing the stump that remained of his leg. I realized that, to them, he was normal, and I began to think that perhaps a child of mine could accept me as I was.

My greater, secret fear was that I'd lose more freedom. In some ways, I realized that having a family might be good. After all, many of my friends were fathers now. Deep inside, I knew that I needed to grow up and take responsibility, even if I was not willing to admit it. So I went along with Karla's wish.

We were not using contraception but Karla didn't become pregnant. Years before, my doctors had told me that it was highly unlikely that I would be able to father children but Karla was adamant that we would be OK. She felt a deep inner certainty that she could not explain.

One day when we travelled to Rookwood Hospital for my regular check-up, we met a new doctor, Dr Buni; he seemed to be kind and helpful and so we had a chat about it.

'Have you thought of having children?' he said.

'Not really,' I replied. 'I thought it would not be possible.'

'Well, there may be ways that we can help you, but we'll have to do some tests first.'

He recommended that I go to Heath Hospital in Cardiff – the same hospital I had been to earlier for an operation after the accident – to see a consultant called Mrs Sheila Walker. Karla and I both underwent tests to see whether we were able to have children. The results were promising but because of my spinal injuries, there were difficulties. The experts decided that we would use artificial insemination by husband (AIH), a relatively new technique in those days, and one that seemed far from straightforward.

I was expected to produce a sperm sample and race off to Heath Hospital with Karla so that she could be inseminated within two hours. The journey to Cardiff took nearly an hour and a half, and then we had to park the car and get to the right department in the huge hospital in time for it to be done. Talk about cutting it fine! The timing had to be right – Karla would have to take her temperature daily to know when she was ovulating. The whole thing was so unnatural and created so much anxiety that I found it impossible to relax and do my side of things.

We talked again to Mrs Walker and she suggested that the hospital should send us a 'home kit' that would arrive in the post. We waited several months, but nothing arrived; eventually we telephoned the hospital. They said that one had been sent to us but that they would send another. We never did find out what had happened to the first kit. Perhaps it went to Bettws in Newport instead of Bettws, Bridgend. If so, then someone in Newport must have had a bit of a surprise in the post one morning!

When the kit finally arrived, we unpacked it eagerly. It was an extremely strange-looking little gadget, and we laughed when we saw it because it seemed impossible that it would work. With little hope that this thing could possibly work, we waited for the right time of the month to use it. As we followed the instructions, we lost even more confidence and in the end could only laugh helplessly at the ludicrousness of what we were doing. What a waste of time! We followed the guidelines though, and Karla stayed in bed for half an hour afterwards and I went off to work feeling strangely depressed. I had warmed to the idea of having a baby of our own, but I couldn't believe that this would work.

Three weeks later, Karla did a home pregnancy test. We waited to see if a black circle appeared on the tester. To our amazement, a black ring began to appear almost straight away and we watched excitedly as it darkened. Karla was pregnant and later, this was confirmed by our doctor. It seemed a miracle that she had conceived at our first inept attempt at using this pathetic little tube!

We were overjoyed. I had told friends that I could not have children and when we announced our news, people were thrilled for us. We rang everyone we knew and told them. I was so pleased, but at the back of my mind I still had a nagging fear; given the extent of my injuries, would our child be normal?

For the first three months, Karla was so unwell that she had to stay in bed: she was sick, unable to eat, and liable to faint if she tried to walk around. After that, she bloomed and loved being pregnant. I was unable to enjoy this time as much as I would have liked, so obsessed was I about the baby's normality. However at the same time, I did spend the months dreaming about watching my son – and I was convinced that it would be a boy – play football. At last, another chance to relive my dream, or so I thought.

Towards the end of her pregnancy, Karla's blood pressure rose alarmingly and she was taken into hospital. No one had told us if we needed to tell the nurses that our child had been conceived by AIH. We weren't sure whether it would make any difference to Karla's treatment. Karla forgot the correct terminology and told the nurse, 'My baby was conceived though AID but my husband is the father. It wasn't a donor.'

The sister must have written AID (Artificial Insemination by Donor) on her notes by mistake, because when the duty doctor came to examine her, he asked her for the name of the father. She was very upset by his words; throughout the pregnancy she had been conscious that people might think that I could not be her baby's father. Little did she realize that when our beautiful baby daughter was born, she would look just like me!

Hayley's arrival proved to be a shock for all of us. It was our fourth wedding anniversary, and I was up at the hospital with Karla for her routine check-up.

'Your waters have broken, Mrs Davies,' said one of the nurses, 'we'll have to keep you in.'

What? But they can't have, it wasn't time. We weren't ready. We looked at each other, hands clasped, in disbelief. I panicked. They called for the doctor immediately.

'I'll just go home for my things,' Karla replied, but the doctor shook his head.

'Your husband will have to do it,' he told her. 'You'll have to stay here in case something happens on the way home.'

I rushed home to fetch Karla's suitcase, pleased to escape from the hospital. I'd had enough of them to last me a lifetime, and coming in with Karla had already proved to be a stressful time. About a month earlier, we had heard one of the other mother's screams as she struggled with her labour. I found this very hard to cope with;

all the memories of being in hospital, and the shouting and screaming I had experienced during my time at Cardiff and Rookwood came flooding back. In the end I panicked and staggered out of the place as fast as I could.

When I came back with Karla's case at about four that afternoon, she was in a room on her own and had been put on a drip because she was not having contractions. Nothing much had happened, and the crisis seemed to have passed. My mind turned to other matters.

'The FA Cup replay is on tonight,' I told her.

'You can go home and watch it, if you like,' she said. 'I'll ring you if anything happens.'

I made my escape, and Dad and I watched the match together. Dad was a great fan of Manchester United, and so we watched the game with excitement.

At half-time I telephoned the hospital to make enquiries about Karla. The nurse replied, 'Your wife and the baby are doing fine.'

'Baby?' I shouted.

'Yes,' said the nurse, 'Mrs Davies has had an emergency Caesarean, but she is doing well.'

Why didn't they phone me sooner? How had I missed my baby's arrival? 'Is it a boy or a girl?' I spluttered.

'Wouldn't you like to find that out when you come down here?' replied the nurse.

I used my best persuasive techniques and the nurse admitted that we had a lovely baby girl.

Dad and Mam were both in the sitting room; they had come to look after me while Karla was in hospital; I told them the news.

'You'll never believe this! We've had a girl.' I sounded disappointed, and in a way I was. A daughter wouldn't be able to become a top class football player. A stupid reaction I know, and one which was completely dispelled when I saw my daughter for the first time.

After the match Dad and I went to the hospital and he was given permission to come in with me, even though this was strictly against the rules. In fact, he saw her before Karla did, because Hayley was taken straight into the special care unit to be checked. He was thrilled to be a grandad.

As soon as I saw my baby daughter, I fell in love with her. She was lovely, with long limbs and perfect features. Karla and I had already chosen a name for her and I murmured it to myself: 'Lydia.'

'She's exactly like you,' said the nurse.

'Thanks,' I replied, feeling relieved that no one could be in any doubt that I really was her father.

Karla was still fast asleep from the anaesthetic so Dad and I decided to go home. Later that evening, the two of us watched a film starring Hayley Mills.

'That's a nice name, boy,' he said.

'I like it, too. It would be a pretty name for my daughter.' I tried it out a few times.

'Yes. All I have to do now is convince Karla!'

I visited Karla next day to find her exhausted but on an emotional high. Still affected by the anaesthetic, she was not really capable of making a decision. Still, I put the idea to her and she agreed, although I don't think she knew what it was that she was agreeing to.

Karla had to stay in hospital for the next ten days. We were deeply grateful to the medical staff; they made sure that Karla had the best care. I visited every day, longing to have my wife and baby home with me.

When the day finally came for them to come home, a nurse carried Hayley to the car and placed her in Karla's arms. At that moment I really felt like a husband and a Dad, and I was proud to introduce little Hayley to my Mam. She had been unable to visit the hospital, and so it was a special moment when she was able to hold her grandchild for the first time.

'It's like holding you all over again, Haydn,' she said tearfully.

Mam and Dad stayed for a week to help Karla adjust. Grateful though we were, we couldn't wait to be alone with our tiny daughter. I would drive home from work each day full of excitement to see her.

Reality soon hit me though. You can't go out whenever you like and you have to take such a lot with you when you do manage to venture out.

For a few months, I enjoyed the novelty of fatherhood, although there were big adjustments for both of us. We soon found out how drastically life changes with the arrival of a baby. Everything takes much longer than it used to, and you have to start planning for things in advance. On top of this, Hayley suffered from night colic and we had plenty of sleepless nights.

I became restless, and started drifting into my old habits, and it didn't take long for me to get back in with the lads. Usually I was first into the pub and last out – and after that I would go on to parties or get food from the local Indian and Chinese restaurants. As before, I often did not arrive home until four or five in the morning. Karla was angry and disappointed. She knew that it was pointless to argue with me when I was drunk, but next day she would tell me exactly what she thought of me. I didn't really care enough to listen to what she said.

'If you don't like it, you can clear off!' I told her.

The truth was that I placed a low value on marriage, and sometimes I did feel like leaving. The major thing that stopped me from leaving was the fear that I wouldn't be able to see Hayley. In her desperate attempts to get me to behave more responsibly, Karla had threatened that if we split up, she would not let me have contact with our baby.

Things came to a head one evening when Hayley was three years old. I staggered home from a works party, noisy, argumentative and extremely drunk, eventually falling flat on the floor and unable to get up.

'Leave me alone,' I shouted repeatedly as Karla tried to get me to my feet and put me to bed. Hayley came from her bedroom, frightened and puzzled.

'What's the matter with Daddy?' she asked, obviously upset, thinking that I had fallen and hurt myself. It suddenly hit me. I was doing this to her! She was now old enough to see me drunk and work out that something was wrong. In fact, because I had come home relatively early, this was the first time that Hayley had seen me in this state, and even in my drunkenness I could sense her fear and confusion. I was so ashamed of what I had done.

For the first time I really understood what the drink was doing to me, to Karla, and now also to Hayley. I vowed that it would be the last time. Surely this had been my wake-up call.

15

THE ANSWER TO EVERYTHING

'I know I've got to get my act together,' I admitted to Karla. 'I'm like a hamster on a wheel; caught in a vicious circle of working all week and being drunk all weekend. There has to be more to life than this.'

'You've said that before,' replied Karla sceptically. 'Nothing ever changes.'

'Yes, but I'm older now.' I struggled to express what I was feeling. 'I'm still behaving like a teenager. I've got a really good wife, a lovely daughter and all the material things I could want, but my life is still empty.' It was such a relief to admit this to her. I had been putting on a front for so long: acting like I was OK, and pretending everything was all right, when I knew it wasn't. In a way I'd been doing this ever since the accident, but I didn't want to pretend any more.

'The only way things are going to change will be if you stop drinking,' she told me. Then she added, 'Maybe it would help if we tried going to church.'

'Church?' I exclaimed.

Church was the last thing I had in mind! I used to get thrown out of RE at school. I hated everything to do with religion: I didn't like hymns, and I didn't understand all of the religious language they used. To me, church was outdated and irrelevant. I wasn't at all interested in any of that. Karla had made this suggestion before but I had always refused bluntly. 'What good would church be?' I had often replied. But she had often brought it up.

When I first met Karla I knew that there was something different about her, but I didn't know what. I didn't know that she was a Christian who had left the church. Gradually I got to know her story. A committed Christian until the age of twenty-one, Karla had gone through a personal crisis and decided that she wanted to see what it was like to live a different way. Almost from the day of our marriage, she'd wanted to return to her faith and to church. And now she was suggesting that this might be the answer to my crisis too!

'I don't mind you going to church if you want to,' I said, 'but you'll have to go on your own, and don't ask me to come with you again.'

But Karla didn't want to go on her own. She was afraid that it would give me an excuse for still more nights out with the boys. Deep down, I began to think that perhaps she was right about church. I also began to wonder whether it was Karla's faith that had carried her through our first few years of marriage.

One day I finally gave in.

'I may as well give it a go. My life is in such a mess that I have nothing to lose. Anyway, for years you've gone everywhere I wanted to go. I owe it to you to go somewhere you want to go, for once.'

This was quite a turnaround for me to actually admit what we both knew to be true. Karla jumped at the chance.

'That's great,' Karla replied, carefully masking her excitement. 'How about next Sunday evening?'

'OK,' I agreed. I was nervous of course, but too macho to admit it. Karla continued. She explained that I couldn't judge a church by this one service and asked if I would attend for a month to give it a fair trial. Reluctantly, I agreed.

So this was it. Haydn Davies agreeing to go to church! I definitely wasn't going to tell my friends. It was all right in the valleys for a girl to go to church – she was a lovely person – but a man – he would be considered a sissy. No, this was going to be something I kept tight-lipped about. Nevertheless, I kept my word.

When we arrived at the local evangelical church, Calfaria Baptist, those people who knew Karla were delighted to see her again and they gave us both a big welcome. One lady, known to everyone as Auntie Syb, said that she had been praying for this day for many years. Apparently she had been praying for me as well as for Karla. I took this with a pinch of salt. How could this lady be praying for me when she didn't know me?

Throughout the service, I felt extremely bored and couldn't wait to get out. An enormously tall man stood at the door, greeting everyone as they left. Although I did not realize it, he was the minister, Reverend David Carey-Jones. He was about six foot five and had a deep voice. He shook my hand and asked me a few questions about myself. I looked up at this gentle giant and thought he must be God. But I still couldn't wait to get out; we were going on to the local disco after church.

'Who is this "Amazing Grace" lady then?' I asked as we got into the car. 'They didn't half go on about her.'

Karla laughed as she explained that 'Amazing Grace' was one of the hymns that we had been singing.

Another week, two men came around with a small piece of bread and a little glass of red liquid.

'What a crabby lot!' I thought. 'They don't give you much to eat!'

Karla whispered, 'You can't have any. Just let it go past.'

'What an insult! They won't even share a bit of bread!' I thought. I didn't want any, anyway. It wasn't enough to feed a sparrow! When we were home, Karla explained that this was all part of communion, and that you could only take it if you were a Christian.

As we went each week, I noticed more and more. There was an old man who would sit at the front; his name was Tom Davies. All through the service he'd be shouting 'Amen!' I felt thoroughly annoyed with him because I thought it was rude. At least I was quiet.

'Stupid old man!' I thought. 'Why doesn't he shut up?'

Later, I discovered that Tom Davies was one of the greatest and godliest men you could ever meet.

I thought the most bizarre people went to this church. There was the man who gave out the books at the door – he frightened me to death. He was about eighty years old, deaf and had one eye. His good eye stared and watered incessantly while the other was permanently closed. Because of his deafness, he spoke strangely. He also had hair growing out of his ears. I used to send Karla in first to get the hymn books! She knew his background; he was actually a sweet-natured and lovely man, who, with his wife had been attending the church for about sixty years.

I was a man of my word and I went to church for a month. It felt like a prison sentence: I had done my time and I certainly did not expect to go back. Shortly after this I had to go into hospital yet again for an operation on my right knee. I was there for about a week before coming home to convalesce.

While I was at home recovering I had a visitor. Karla showed him in and I saw that it was the six foot five giant I had met at church. I wasn't sure who he was, so I called him the Vicar Man. Karla had tried to explain that he was the pastor, but to me pasta was a plate of food. I couldn't understand all of this strange terminology. Pastor Carey-Jones stayed for about half an hour and seemed interested in me and how I was doing.

After he left, I told Karla 'It was really nice of that Vicar Man to come and visit.' Then after a moment more I continued, 'Just to repay him for his kindness, and to thank God for my beautiful little daughter, I will be really good and go to church once more.'

I had to wait two months until my leg was out of plaster before I could keep my word, and by that time it was late autumn in 1985. This was going to be the last time I went, and I didn't want Karla to be under any illusions. I still thought it was boring, but for some reason, after the service I found myself telling Karla, 'I'm going to be really, really good to you now and stay until Christmas. Then I'm off! No more after that!'

This would compensate for all that I had put her through. During this time I stopped resisting church and got on with my stint of attendance.

'While I'm here,' I thought, 'I might as well try to listen.' But it was still all Double Dutch to me. I noticed that most other people were listening intently and enjoying the service. Why were they finding it so exciting when I was so bored? What was I missing?

After church one evening, an old lady called Mrs Gough asked whether I wanted to come to a fellowship meeting one Saturday evening. I still didn't know why they used all these strange terms, and I didn't know what she meant. I said I'd go along anyway though, to see what it was like. Then it suddenly dawned upon me. Saturday night after the match was of course when the boys would be going out to have a good time. Here I was going to a fellowship meeting! But I said I would go, and I intended to keep to my word.

We went along and Mrs Gough let us in. The place was full of old people, and nearly all women, too. I sat next to Auntie Syb, who I recognized as the church organist. The more I chatted to her, the more I liked her and wanted to learn from her. I came to realize that these religious people were normal people who loved God. However I was convinced that I would never be like them, I was so different. And, as I kept reminding myself, this was Saturday night . . .

'There is no way I'm staying here all night,' I promised myself. 'I'll stay for about an hour and then shoot off down the pub.'

I thought that nobody would miss me. But to my utter amazement, whenever I tried to get up and leave, I found that I was unable to move. It wasn't just that I was being lazy, or that my legs were stiff, I really could not move.

At around 10:30 I tried again.

'I'll be off now and catch last orders,' I thought, but still I couldn't get up. What was it that was stopping me from going?

We stayed there until two in the morning and in the end there was just Karla, me, and Mrs Gough. We heard all about her life. She'd become a Christian not long after her marriage and for 45 years, she had prayed for her husband to become one too. He worked in the colliery and was as tough and as hardened as any of the men that went down the pit. She kept praying for him over all those years and then he had an amazing conversion experience and there was a dramatic change in his life. I did wonder what she meant by conversion experience but continued to listen. For the final five years of their marriage she said they were able to share their faith together.

'Our first prayer together was sweeter than our first kiss,' said Mrs Gough.

'Really?' I thought, 'How could that work?' I didn't say anything though.

As we were leaving the house in the early hours of the morning she said, 'Haydn, make sure you put yourself right with God, because he has brought you out of that car crash for a reason.'

Now this really touched me. What did she mean 'right with God'? How could she talk about the car crash like that? I had always wondered why I had survived when the others were killed and now I could not stop thinking about the old lady's words. Why had I stayed at her house until two in the morning? What had kept me there? Was it the fact that these people were so different from me, that they had something that I had not yet experienced? As we left, I asked Karla to explain more to me about the Christian life.

We sat up talking for most of the rest of the night. Karla explained many things about Christianity to me. I tried to grasp them, but couldn't: salvation, repentance, forgiveness, why did there have to be such big words? I struggled to get my head round them all. Karla told me somewhere in the conversation that God could break down the resistance of the hardest heart. I beat my fist on my chest. 'There is no way He is going to break this heart.' I was not a bitter person, but had become very toughened as a result all the horrific things that I had been through and seen in hospital. I didn't fear anyone, even God.

The next day we went to church in the evening as usual. As I listened to the preacher, I felt uncomfortable, and squirmed in my seat. I wondered why this preacher was looking at me all the time, and how he knew so much about me. Had someone told him? He was saying things that I thought somebody must have told him about my life. I now know that it was the Holy Spirit, convicting me of my sins, and speaking directly to me.

I realized that Jesus Christ was speaking to me. He knew about me, knew what I had done, knew what I thought; He knew everything. I believe He was saying 'Haydn Davies, you carry your cross and follow me.' I had fought hard against it, with all my pride and determination, but something in my heart wanted to respond now; to sincerely say sorry for all the wrong things I had done. I knew then that I wanted to follow Jesus. And so this is what I did, I prayed for the first time. 'Lord Jesus, I know that I am a sinner. Please forgive me for my sins. Please make me into a new person like you say you will. Amen.' Immediately I felt peace inside, I felt clean.

I realized then that God had broken my hard resistant heart. I was a new person. No one told me this; I just knew that I was changed inside.

After the service, when I told the others what I'd prayed, they hugged and kissed me. This was too much and made me very uncomfortable. I didn't understand why they were making such a fuss. However, when Karla and I got home, she explained to me the importance of what I'd done.

'You've been saved, Haydn. Without Jesus, you would have gone to hell, but now you have a place in heaven. You have become a Christian. You remember we talked about this before. God has changed you.'

It was true. In October 1985 in Calfaria Baptist church, I repented of my sin and committed my life to Jesus. He was now my Lord and my Saviour. If someone had told me that they had done this and that they now felt peace, contentment and joy, I would have laughed at them. However I realized that only God could change people, and only God could change me. And this is how I felt – content and at peace. I just knew that my life had changed.

A NEW WAY OF LIVING

Had I really been saved? Could it be that God had forgiven my sins? Or was yesterday a dream? I woke up excited but unsure. Of course it had happened and I did feel like a burden had been lifted. Karla smiled when I told her how I felt.

'You've made a big decision and commitment, but it's the best decision that you could ever make.'

I knew it was. And I knew my life would have to change. I soon found solid evidence that what had happened to me was real and lasting. I used to swear a lot, being an ex-footballer and a factory worker. Now, every time I tried to swear, nothing would come out!

I carried on going to church every Sunday and started attending the prayer meeting on Tuesdays. Although I was still going to the pubs and clubs, gradually I felt less happy there and I felt like I didn't belong. I was more at home with the Christians; the danger was however that I thought I was a really good Christian, attending church and prayer meeting. It was almost as if I were doing God a favour. I still had a lot to learn about my new faith.

Karla and I began to pray together every night, an exciting new experience for me. I wanted so much to used to call himself 'The Lone Ranger', making a joke of it, but it must have been difficult for him when everyone else was with his or her spouse. He never criticised Mam and would defend her when the family put pressure on her to try to go out more. 'Leave her alone,' he would say, 'she does her best and I'm proud of her.'

He appreciated her qualities as a housewife: keeping the house spotless and preparing his meals faithfully. She was extremely house proud and never let the house go, even if she did neglect her appearance. It took commitment for him to stay in the marriage. He couldn't go on holiday and he could only go out on Friday evenings if someone sat with her. Many men would have left her, but Dad never wavered in his devotion.

In my favourite memory of him, I see him with Karla and me in our new property. We had some of the family round, to help us move in and my cousin walked into the glass patio doors, not realizing that the door was closed. He staggered backwards, clutching his face rather comically while we laughed. Dad literally collapsed on the floor, almost crying with laughter, and was still laughing when he went home for his tea. He had a natural gift for making people chuckle and if I was having one of my bad days, he could always make me feel better. I saw him nearly every day, and of course he had been there with me in hospital. Dad had been my constant support. He would fix anything that was broken and often came to see us to get a break from home.

Football was his life and he watched every game he could on television. Mam usually went to bed at about seven o'clock and he'd be on his own, watching sport. I'd often come round and he'd be wide-eyed, concentrating intently on the game. 'I love my football, see, boy!' he would say.

I turned to Karla and Alan in the waiting room. I felt a peace that seemed overwhelmingly supernatural. Some time later, the surgeon and a nurse came to tell us that Dad had died during the operation. He had had an aneurysm.

'I'm extremely sorry,' the nurse said.

I replied that I was all right because I was a Christian and had God's peace.

'I wish I had what you have,' the nurse replied.

We now had to face breaking the news to my Mam and my daughter. My aunt and uncle had also come to the hospital and they went home to tell Mam while we stayed to see Dad one last time.

The next few days were the most difficult days of my life, even in comparison to all that had happened to me. It was my first taste of real grief. Although I shed many, many tears, our little family still had this supernatural peace. However what I dreaded most of all was Dad's funeral. On the night before, Karla, Hayley and I were sitting together singing Christian hymns, experiencing God's comfort. And during the funeral service itself, God's presence was very real to me, as if His arms were around me. As I travelled in the funeral car following the hearse, I felt strong and calm, almost as if I were floating on air. God carried me through it all in perfect peace.

God never promises to shield us from pain and upset, but He is with us in it – as He was with me during this time. As he says in Joshua 1:5, 'I will never leave you nor forsake you.' And we did know and feel this to be true in the years to follow.

21

THE GOD WHO ANSWERS PRAYER

Not long ago, I was walking through my house with a glass of water in my hand. I am unsteady on my feet, to say the least, and I had a stick in the other hand. There is a step down from the kitchen to the study and I lost my balance and dropped the glass. It shattered. As I slipped on the water and began to fall, the stick flew out of my hand. I screamed, knowing that I was falling onto the broken glass. There was no one in the house to help me deal with the bleeding wounds that I would suffer. Because of my disability, I wouldn't even be able to get up without going onto my hands and knees among the needle-sharp shards of glass. All this happened so fast that there was not even time to pray. But the expected impact onto the floor and the glass didn't happen! When I was three quarters of the way down, I seemed to be lifted up and set on my feet again.

I knew something remarkable – miraculous in fact, had happened. 'Thank you, Lord,' I breathed, as I sat in my study and recovered from my fright.

I remembered other times when God came to the rescue. One of these took place when Karla, Hayley and I were driving towards the village of Llanharan to do some shopping. Rounding a bend, we were horrified to see a car heading towards us at speed, driving on the wrong side of the road. Instinctively, we braced ourselves for the impact, since there was no way of avoiding a head-on collision. The car was only yards from us. On the other side of the road, in the lane that the driver should have been using, four cars were bunched together, nose to tail. There was simply nowhere for this rogue car to go.

'He thinks he's on a dual carriageway!' The realization came as I waited for the impact. Suddenly, miraculously, the car pulled over. It was like watching a cartoon where things can fit into impossible spaces. To our shocked minds the car seemed to have disappeared into thin air. Incredibly, the road was clear.

Thinking that this was it, we were astonished.

'Did that really happen?' I asked.

'Angels were looking after us there,' Karla said breathlessly. 'That had to be divine intervention.'

There was another time when Hayley was still young and our family was on holiday in Devon. As usual, Karla was at the wheel as we took a scenic drive through a forest. Dusk was falling, and it started to rain heavily.

'It's getting late,' Karla said. 'I think we had better get back to the hotel.' So we started to make our way back, but in the gathering gloom we seemed to be driving in circles. We simply could not find our way out of the forest. Karla began to pray silently for help. As she did so, a Range Rover came into view in the distance, as if from nowhere. Relieved at this sign of human life, Karla followed it. Suddenly it disappeared from sight and we found ourselves on the main road.

'Strange!' Karla said. 'I can't see that car any more. Where's it gone? It can't have arrived at the main road before us or we would have seen it.' As she thought about this incident, she became more and more convinced that this had been another encounter with an angel.

Before these experiences I had been a little sceptical about angelic interventions. However, Scripture says that 'some have entertained angels without knowing it' (Hebrews 13:2). It also says that angels are ministering spirits sent to serve those who will inherit salvation (1:14). Looking back now I wonder if there have been moments when angels have ministered to me when I have been completely unaware of their presence. I do know though that nothing is impossible with God.

Some years ago when Hayley was still a small child, she fell from the garden wall. By late afternoon, her temperature had begun to rise and she had such a headache that she could not bear the daylight in her eyes. Karla became worried and telephoned the doctor. He came and examined Hayley straight away.

'I'm not sure what this is,' he told us. 'I don't think it can have been caused by falling from a wall. I'll give her some antibiotics straight away, but it would be a good idea to take her into hospital. I'll call an ambulance.'

'I'll take her by car,' Karla told him, very worried now. 'It will be quicker.'

'All right,' replied the doctor. 'I'll give you a note to take to casualty with you.'

While they were waiting in the casualty area, Hayley vomited. Because her temperature was still high, the emergency doctor decided to admit her to hospital for observation and tests and she spent several days on the children's ward.

By now, it was clear that she was very ill indeed. It proved impossible to bring down her dangerously high temperature, even though she was almost naked on a hospital bed with a fan directed on her. We suspected that it was meningitis. We were frightened, of course, although we did not fully realize at the time how close Hayley actually came to dying. Karla was unable to stay with her at night because she was also caring for me and she felt deeply torn when Hayley begged her not to leave. Desperately anxious, we decided to telephone as many of our Christian friends as possible and ask them to pray. They did, and when Karla returned to the hospital, she learnt that our daughter's temperature had suddenly returned to normal.

We look back on that time as an amazing encounter with God. We were focused on the urgency of the problem, but God was present with us. Somehow I knew that God was in control and I had peace in the midst of the anxiety – it's hard to explain it, but that's how it was. I felt as if I was being carried, but it was only later that I realized the extent to which God's power supported us in that crisis. This happened at a time when I did not know the Scriptures or much about doctrine; I was a new Christian. With Karla, I could only cling to God in simple faith. But sometimes that it is all that is required.

I have learnt in prayer that we do not always get what we ask for, as we have to pray in line with God's will. I try and make Jesus' prayer in Gethsemane my own: 'Yet not what I will, but what you will.' We have seen some wonderful answers to prayer though. I prayed for my friend Rob when he was seriously ill in hospital and knew inwardly that my prayers for his healing were answered. Another friend, Paul, was also very ill yet when I prayed for him he didn't recover and he died. I can't explain why it is God's will to heal some and not others; I just accept that He is in control of all things.

Another example of prayer leading to a very different outcome is when we thought God was calling us to move near Bath. This was at the time when Steve became the minister of his church, and we used to frequently visit him and the family. During this time we got to know the people of that church really well, especially the youth. As time went on we felt we were part of their family, and that maybe God was calling us to move there as Hayley, now fifteen, had made so many new Christian friends her own age. We even went on their church summer holiday to Geneva on two occasions.

These were great adventures. The best part of the holidays for me was not only having constant Christian fellowship, or taking in the beautiful scenery, but actually seeing Calvin's church, his pulpit, and the Reformers' Wall.

Throughout this time we continued to pray about moving to Bath and put our bungalow on the market. The hardest part was finding the right time to tell my Mam about it; she would think that we were abandoning her. We had taken care of her since my Dad had died. We knew that in all things it was right to put God first, and to our astonishment she took it extremely well.

We needn't have worried. As it turned out, our bungalow did not sell, but we kept on praying. We looked at some properties in the Bath area, and realized that the prices were far beyond our reach. It seemed hopeless. With Hayley about to start her GCSEs we put the possible move on hold. Realizing that God, for now had closed the door for Bath, we looked at properties in the Bridgend area; by now we had been attending Litchard Mission Church, Bridgend for six years. 'This will be a stepping stone until our circumstances change and we will be much closer to church,' we told each other.

Housing prices are higher in the town and we found that we could not afford a bungalow. Our estate agent showed us a small house and although it was not really what we had been looking for, we sensed at once that it was God's will for us. We bought it, telling each other again, 'This is only for a time. God will show us when He is ready to give us the next part of His plan. Maybe in time this property will increase enough in value for us to be able to afford something in Bath.'

I was finding it more difficult to walk and climb stairs as I grew older and we knew that we would soon need a bungalow. We prayed about this for about a year and considered the options available to us.

'Perhaps we should buy a plot of land,' Karla said one day, about a year later. 'We could build our own bungalow. Every time we try to look at a suitable property, it is either too expensive or sold before we can even view it. We do need to have everything on one floor though so that you can manage more easily.'

We decided that God had something for us and we were patient. Then we learnt that a small bungalow belonging to a member of our church (and right opposite the church gates) was empty because she had gone into a residential home. Should we consider it or was God calling us to Bath?

'I'd love to live there,' I told Karla. 'I could get to church easily and with so many of our friends passing the gate, we'd have plenty of visitors. Let's find out if we can buy it.'

'Someone else has already agreed to buy it,' she replied. 'I made enquiries today.'

'Well, let's carry on praying. If it is God's will that bungalow will be ours – and, if not, God will provide something much better.'

So we continued to ask God for His will to be done. One Sunday, as we drove to church, Karla said, 'I just know that that bungalow is ours.' And I believed her.

We went to church as usual and left the issue in God's hands. On that same evening, we got a call from the vendor:

'The other buyer has dropped out because he thinks you need the bungalow more than he does, are you still interested?' Of course we were! We gave a definite yes, agreed a price, and eventually made the move. Yes, God does answer prayers.

22

A DIFFICULT YEAR

Mam's lifelong struggle with illness meant that my grandmother became like a second mum to me. She did so much, taking me on holiday and excursions. I called them both Mam – and I lost them both within three weeks; 2004 was a horrible year. I learnt more about grieving in that year than I had in the whole of my life up to then.

My Gran was an extrovert, always laughing and joking; the star of any gathering. Everyone loved her. Nothing got her down and she was so generous that she would give away her last penny. She had over twenty grandchildren and more than thirty great-grandchildren and she remembered every birthday and marked it with a card and gift. In her latter days, she became deaf and almost blind, but she still went out and she still laughed. I told her often that I was praying for her.

'What are you paying for now?' she would ask, much to my amusement.

Happy to feel useful, she would clean my Mam's house for her when Mam was ill, despite Mam's protests. 'No one cleans my house for me!' But we knew that she couldn't do it herself, and it proved impossible to stop

Gran from doing this. Even when she could barely see what she was doing Gran was there cleaning – and managing to spill bleach all over the carpet.

Gran lived alone until she was ninety-four and spent her last months in a residential home. Karla and I visited her a week or so before she died and had a very special time with her. However, she looked so frail and old that I began to cry; she was dying and there was nothing I could do. I loved her so much, and she meant such a lot to me.

'Don't be upset,' she told me. 'God is looking after me.'

I was thrilled with this expression of faith. She had always respected my faith and liked me to sing hymns to her. She was part of a generation that respected and believed in God and probably would have had less of a culture shock in going to church than I did. A week or so later, she died – her body simply shut down. There were hundreds at her funeral. This shows the kind of person Gran was.

Meanwhile Mam was already ill. She had begun to deteriorate when my grandmother went into a care home. They had spoken on the telephone every day until then, but this became impossible once Gran was in residential care. My Mam worried about her until she became ill herself, feeling guilty because her agoraphobia prevented her from visiting Gran. For months, Mam had a chest infection that simply would not clear up and within a week of the funeral she was taken into hospital, unable to breathe. She hated that, and would have done anything to stay at home.

Mam had had TB when she was young which left a shadow on one of her lungs. The other lung had had to compensate and now this, too, began to fail. She deteriorated to the point where she had to be taken straight into intensive care. There an oxygen mask was fastened over her face so tightly that it broke her skin. I can't imagine what this must have been like for her in her condition, but she was very brave. The chest infection did not improve despite the antibiotics she was given, and she continued to deteriorate, until she developed pneumonia. As a last resort, her doctors decided to intubate her; maybe her lungs would begin to heal once they were given a rest. When Karla heard about this, she rushed to the hospital. She wanted to speak to Mam before she was so sedated that conversation would be impossible.

She tried to reassure Mam and said, 'Don't worry. Once they put the tube in, your lungs will begin to get better. Trust in Jesus.'

Mam was unable to speak because of the mask, but she managed to say, 'I'm all right,' and she put her hands together as if she were praying. Karla felt that Mam was telling her that she was indeed trusting Jesus. We had been warned of the dangers, and knew that there was a possibility that Mam's lungs would refuse to work once the tube was removed. We visited every day, and every day she would have blood tests and an x-ray. Things only got worse, though, and by the end of the week, her doctor called us aside.

'There's nothing more we can do for her. We have tried everything we know. We feel that we are now prolonging death, rather than saving life. We don't want to give any more treatment.'

Karla and I agonised over the decision. After some thought and prayer, and consultation with my brother, we agreed to it. Two doctors would have to sign for the removal of treatment, and it would be confirmed on the following Monday. They assured us that they'd keep her comfortable and reduce her oxygen level to that of a normal room.

We asked how long Mam would survive after this was done.

'It won't be days, more like hours, but she could survive for up to a day. We won't do anything until you are present so that you and other close family members can be with her at the end.'

We telephoned members of the family, giving them the news. Then I spent Sunday contemplating the fact that, the following day, my Mam was going to die. That evening, Hayley and I went to the hospital to spend some time with her. We stayed for about two hours, shedding tears at first, talking to her and reminiscing as if she could hear us. Perhaps she could; anyway, it was a special, comforting time. Mam seemed to respond, opening her eyes from time to time as if she knew that we were there and understood what we were saying. We left feeling sad but peaceful.

The next day, I dressed and got ready to go out, knowing that I was going to watch my Mam die. It was my first experience of seeing someone die in front of me. As we arrived, our pastor walked through the door. Pastor Chris Jenkins read from the Bible and prayed and we sang a Christian song. I could see that the nurses were moved by this.

We went to the waiting room while the medical staff prepared Mam and reduced the oxygen level and then we were called back to her bedside. By this time, my aunt had joined us. I stroked Mam's hair and kissed her.

Within ten minutes, she had died, very peacefully. We weren't even aware that it had happened until the nurse told us. It was not the long-drawn out experience that it might have been and we were grateful to God for that.

Again, more waiting. We had to go to the waiting room while the tube was removed and her body was laid out, and then we were told that we could stay with her for as long as we wished. Once again God had been with us, He'd simply carried me through. I knew that God was in charge. The peace sustained me through my Mam's funeral. The funeral itself, conducted by Pastor Chris, was a wonderful celebration of the Christian hope of heaven. No more pain, no more suffering – I couldn't wait to get there!

Yet here I was, numbed for the close deaths of my Gran and Mam. The stress and shock threw me into a deep, reactive depression. I'm an extrovert like my Gran. I have usually managed, despite pain and weakness, to create a cheerful and good-humoured atmosphere around me and to engage in banter and fun. Now, all this left me and I also succumbed to a chest infection that pulled me down still further. I couldn't go on. I was grieving for my Mam, my Gran, and for my Dad who had died some years before. It was overwhelming; I felt like I had been orphaned. I was lost and depressed; memories of the accident came flooding back. I'd not felt this bad since my time in hospital just after the accident. During those early years, yes, I had contemplated suicide; and sometimes even to this day my emotions can be all over the place, especially when I'm in pain. During the six months after Mam's death, I felt so ill that I decided I was ready to die; I was tired of the fighting that I had done for the last 31 years since that night out with the boys. Couldn't it all end now?

23

PAIN MY COMPANION

I was ready to die, but God had other ideas, and as the months went by I began to come to terms with the deaths of my two 'Mams'. My physical condition also began to improve and the persistent chest infection gradually improved. I began to be able to see things in perspective again.

God had been faithful, but so had Karla: a real rock for me during these difficult times. She is the most patient and understanding person imaginable, and I tell her all my problems.

Life is still hard though, and sometimes people say to me: 'This God that you serve can't be so great or He wouldn't let you suffer as you do. Why doesn't He heal you?'

My response? *I would not change a thing.* I would prefer to be in pain every day rather than not be a Christian, and would willingly go through it all again if that is what it took. Suffering is only for a short while. As a woman suffers in labour for a while to experience the joy of having a baby, so I know that my suffering is temporary; I will soon be in heaven where there is so much to look forward to.

I love telling everybody about Jesus and when I'm doing that, I forget about the pain because I am so thrilled with the news I am sharing. I have never prayed to be healed. I believe that I can be used more by God the way I am now. I cannot rely on my own strength and this makes me more dependent on God.

When Jesus was at His weakest on the cross, He did His greatest work. When the apostle Paul was in prison, he also did some of his greatest work, writing letters to the churches and encouraging them. John Bunyan wrote *Pilgrim's Progress* in prison. When I'm at my weakest, God truly uses me in great power. When I have no energy or strength, suddenly I'm full of power. Saint Paul wrote in 2 Corinthians 12:10, 'When I am weak, then I am strong.' And I'm reminded again and again of that truth. My circumstances don't really allow me to forget it!

When I was in Cardiff Royal Infirmary, in traction, one of the nurses would sit at the side of my bed, reading to me. One night, she said, 'I'm going to tell you something off the record. When you get out of here, you are going to need some help, some counselling, to help you re-adjust your life.' Then she added, 'Your mind will never adapt to your body. It will want to do things that your body can't.'

I didn't really understand what she meant by this until I was discharged and tried to watch football matches. Then it hit me; I would never be able to play again. This was heartbreaking for me. Sometimes in the middle of a match I would have to leave, because of the longing I felt to get on the pitch and play. For years I grieved over this, knowing that I would never again run along the field with the roar of the crowd in my ears or send the ball rocketing towards the goal. I'd had a taste of it, but now it was taken from me. Having this snatched from me was like having my heart torn out; would I survive?

It was twelve years before I got over the pain of being unable to play football – and I only came to terms with it when I became a Christian. What Jesus Christ accomplished on the cross involved my complete salvation on every level and that included the aching loss of my football career. If faith can't work on this practical level, then it can't work at all.

I hope you've seen that at the same time, my objectives in life changed. Where once football had been my life, Christ took its place. I wanted different things and although I still enjoy football, it is a hobby now and not an obsession – much to my wife's delight!

So what is it like having pain as my companion? On every single night for over thirty years, I have been in severe pain. I have serious damage to my nerve endings and I also suffer from muscle spasms and incontinence. For twenty-five years, I did not sleep for more than two or three hours a night. I would wake in the mornings feeling exhausted, physically and mentally. It is always worse in the night; I have too much time to dwell on things. Poor Karla. I would try to keep her talking for as long as possible because when she went to sleep I felt profoundly lonely. When I became a Christian, I began to pray and read the Bible during the night which did help, despite my poor concentration caused by the medication that I have to take to relax my nerves and muscles.

Now I take sleeping tablets, although I still only get about six hours sleep. Combined with my other medication, they make me slow, especially in the mornings, and I have to take the day at my own pace.

So much of my life has been frustrating, more so maybe than if I had been permanently in a wheelchair, because of the constant decisions and choices involved. Worse, I feel as if my dignity has been taken away.

Wherever I go, I feel that people are looking at me. Even at the best of times, I feel incomplete and inferior as a man. As mentioned already, I'm also finding it more difficult to walk. As a result, I'm beginning to feel happier and more relaxed in a wheelchair – at least I know I will get from one place to the next without struggle. But I still have inhibitions about being seen in the chair by people I know. Counselling in the early days might have helped me deal with these things better. Perhaps I would have dealt with marriage better. I sometimes wonder why Karla married me and often feel that I'm a burden to her. Planning is difficult because I don't know until the day whether or not I will be well enough to go somewhere.

My worst problem is incontinence. I have only two minutes after I realize that I need to empty my bladder. Wherever I go, I'm tense because I have to make sure that I'm not too far from a toilet and sometimes I have to wear incontinence pads. I have had many 'accidents'. I find all this humiliating and embarrassing and it is difficult to explain it to anyone.

I don't want to tell you all this to make you feel sorry for me; I simply want to paint an honest picture. In some ways, I wish I could hide all these problems from people, especially when it comes to public speaking. One major reason that I become very nervous when I am asked to speak in meetings is that I am afraid that I will be publicly humiliated by these problems. Yet God has never let me down and I never refuse an invitation to speak. The devil does tempt me to give up, asking 'Why should you put yourself through all this?' I battle against it, and it has sometimes led me to have panic attacks. These are awful experiences when I want to run away, yet I know there is nowhere to run and I feel as though the whole room is closing in on me. People are talking yet I cannot hear them and I feel desperate. Often I am asked to speak at men's breakfasts or as an after-dinner speaker; this is particularly difficult as I have to try to eat first and control my physical system over quite a period of time before I finally get up to speak. However, once I am on my feet and speaking, God's power strengthens me and I never have a problem.

There is a saying, 'No pain, no gain,' and I feel that I have learnt the truth of this. I have to persevere through the pain to gain the will and inspiration from God to speak. When I have finished speaking, I simply can't wait to do it all over again!

And what about my family? How does it affect them? My patience sometimes snaps, and I go into my study to be quiet when I know that I might lose my self-control. I have not always been good at disclosing to them that I am in pain and they have felt rejected when I have shut myself away instead of spending time with them. 'Sorry, it's just my way of dealing with it,' I have had to explain. Nowadays, I try to be more open about how I am feeling.

Until recently, I didn't realize just how much it had affected Hayley. For seven years, my Hayley was a student working hard, and during that time I felt that I couldn't tell her off because of the stress she was under. I recently told her that from now on I would be straight with her. She replied, 'Dad, I appreciate this. I've also had to be very careful in the way that I've dealt and spoken to you, because of your pain.'

Quite often, we are late for meetings, and sometimes we fail to arrive. I fight to be able to go to church and sometimes I lose the battle. Unfortunately, as I grow older, these problems become worse.

Of course there are times when I do not feel like getting up in the morning. Pain distorts my thinking and on a number of occasions, I have gone to bed and asked God if I can come home to heaven. Joni Eareckson has written about this. She describes how she wakes up on some mornings feeling that she cannot face another day and she prays to God, asking for grace to accept her problems.

I also deal with pain through prayer. When I am feeling stronger, I read the Bible and Christian books. I find great comfort in the writings of the Puritan Thomas Watson, whose words often touch my heart. Charles Haddon Spurgeon, the nineteenth century preacher, is often called 'the prince of preachers.' He suffered with severe gout and depression, and would sometimes collapse in the pulpit through exhaustion. Yet thousands came to hear him preach and he spoke in the power of the Holy Spirit. He wrote five hundred letters a week and nearly a hundred books in his life! When he died at fifty-seven, still serving God, thousands had been converted through his ministry. There are many others, known and less well-known, who have suffered in their own ways, and yet this suffering has been for the glory of God. When I think of this, the mist clears and I can see the rainbow. Pain is my temporary companion yes, but God is my constant companion.

24

A HAND ON MY SHOULDER

'You must be joking!'

I hate having my photograph taken, never mind being filmed. When the suggestion was made that a film should be made about my life I didn't know how to respond.

'Of my life?'

It happened when I'd been in contact with a woman who was applying for a job with a Norwegian Christian television company. Needing to find some Christian testimonies to use during her interview, she rang me and asked if I could tell her my story over the phone.

I waited for almost a year without hearing whether the filming would be pursued. Actually, I was relieved because the thought of having my face beamed all around the world intimidated me. We're all like the prophet Jonah sometimes, who ran away from what God told him to do. But God didn't want this to go away. A good friend of mine, Mike Curnow, knew the couple who produced the videos for the company. Mike recommended me to them and a few weeks later I had another phone call. My story was going to be filmed during the next few months!

When I heard the news, I remembered the time a few years before when I felt God saying that He would use me in a special way when I was forty-six; I had now reached that age. Could this be it?

In May 2001, Barbara and Terry Page brought their crew to my home, and within an hour it resembled a television studio. There were lights, cameras and screens everywhere, and we had to keep the windows shut to keep everyday noises out. It was so hot! The whole thing was a bit bewildering, but when the time came for filming to begin, Barbara sat near me, prompting and helping me.

I had told my story on many occasions but this time I froze. The camera was right on me and the microphone seemed down my throat. After struggling for about five minutes, I asked if we could stop. I wanted to start again. Terry suggested that we have a time of prayer first, and then he put his hand on my shoulder and prayed. I felt uneasy about this style of praying but I could not really stop him since he was the man in charge. When we started filming again, however, there was an amazing difference! I was able to speak with authority; words seemed to fly out of my mouth and I spoke freely for two hours.

The film was broadcast from Norway into Asia and Africa. Certain words that might be offensive to Muslims were banned. For example, I could not say the words Christian, or Church or Christmas. As you can imagine, this made things rather difficult, and I had to do a few re-takes before I got it right. Filming went on for most of the day and I was exhausted by the end of it. The company wanted to film me in my wheelchair but because I was embarrassed to be seen in it in the street, they had to film me indoors. It was a lovely, special day. Barbara and Terry were lovely people: warm, caring and very godly.

The next step was for the material to be edited into a twenty-minute video; a process that would take some months. There was some debate between the British company and the Norwegian company about what should be left in. When the video came out nearly a year later, Terry phoned to tell me that it was ready, and he put two or three copies in the post so that he could have my comments.

We were overwhelmed by the accuracy and realism of it. The car crash made our stomachs churn and Hayley cried as she saw what I had been through. I was a little disappointed that certain things had been left out but when Karla and I prayed about it, we felt peace that God had put in what He wanted.

This was only the beginning. I was excited when Terry told me that the story had been a great success in Africa and Asia – so much so that we thought it could also be used in Britain. I showed it to many of my friends, who were excited about it too. They agreed that it would be a good way of showing people what Jesus had done in my life.

Karla and I ordered a hundred copies, hoping to distribute my testimony to as many people as possible. Inspired by the singer and songwriter, Keith Green, who didn't want to charge for his songs, we chose to give the videos away. After all, why should people have to pay to hear about Jesus? Some people did give a donation and this money covered most of the cost. Within a few months the videos had all gone.

At this point, our church became involved. They decided to help us distribute the video and took over the financial aspect, although they weren't trying to make a profit. Since then, people have begun to use it in youth meetings and church services, and a number of people have been deeply challenged after watching it. Some teachers have used it as part of a GSCE teaching pack to help students think about religious experiences. The pack was put together by Linda Jenkins, who also arranged for me to speak to the students at the school where she was head of RE. This was a great opportunity, and I was able to have some interesting conversations. Now, whenever I tell my story at services and speaking engagements, I take copies with me so that more people are able to watch the video. It's also available as a DVD now. I don't make any money out of this. My aim is to tell as many people as possible the good news about Jesus.

I also gave a copy to most of my family. Their response was very positive, although many of them are not Christians. My brother-in-law, who likes to see things done properly, commented that the video was well-made and that he was impressed by the way I spoke on it. Little did he know about the importance of prayer and how God's power had carried me through! Other family members responded by commenting on the amazing resemblance between me and the actor who played me as a young man. These weren't professional actors, just some lads from Terry Page's local church who had volunteered; but they did an amazingly good job.

I often wonder about what might have been if that June night had ended differently. On the day before the video was filmed, I felt depressed and I drove up to the football field near where I lived, the one that I used to practise on. Back then I had felt fit and good, and didn't need others to tell me that I had potential; I *knew* it. Thousands might have come to my matches and millions might have watched me on television. But there was an irony here. The accident had happened, and because of it millions of people worldwide would now be able to watch the story of my life!

Recently, someone asked me if I had ever been bitter about my accident and disability.

'Bitter?' I responded. 'How could I be bitter when it has brought such spiritual riches in my life? I'm glad that I broke my neck and I would go through it all again rather than be fit and not have Jesus in my life.'

People think I'm crazy to say this. Reading it you might think that too; but consider this: how many of the people in your favourite football team could you name? What about the team of five years ago, or ten years ago, or even fifty years ago? What about your national team? Sports stars come and go, especially on the international stage. Think of David Beckham, a brilliant player who went from England captain to being dropped from the team after the World Cup in 2006. For every player the day comes when they leave the pitch for the last time, and it's over; that day came very early for me but I've not finished – there's more to come for me.

Bill Shankly, football legend and Liverpool's greatest ever manager, delivered perhaps the most famous quote in football. He said, 'Some people believe football is a matter of life and death. I'm very disappointed with that attitude; I can assure you it's much, much more than that.'

Maybe he's right, maybe football means more to some people than life and death, but I know something even more valuable. When all the matches have been played and football is gone forever, when there's no more gambling, no more beer, no more nights out with the boys, what good is glory on the field to them now? Some of the men that I played against have since died. Where are they now? I know that I will be in heaven with Jesus, completely healed and fully restored.

This is why I'm telling you my story. A night out with the boys had devastating consequences, yes, but it brought me into a living relationship with Jesus Christ. Perhaps you have questions, perhaps like me you have made many mistakes and have regrets. That's OK. God wants to forgive and restore you and make your life mean something, forever, if only you will let Him. Jesus said 'I am the way and the truth and the life' (John 14:6). All you need to do is put your trust in Jesus, and you will come to realize as I have, that life will *never* be complete without Jesus.

Further Information

If you would like to know more about the Christian life and what it means to be a Christian then please do contact the author at the following web address:
www.haydn-davies.co.uk

Resources

Haydn's testimony and life story is also available on video and DVD. If you are interested in purchasing a copy for you or your church then please contact Litchard Mission Church:

LMC,
c/o Haydn Davies,
1 Hubert Drive,
Litchard,
Bridgend
CF31 1PW
Tel: 01656 663371
Email: lmc@haydn-davies.co.uk